new loft living

First published in the United States of America in 2002
by UNIVERSE PUBLISHING
A Division of Rizzoli International Publications, Inc.
300 Park Avenue South
New York, NY 10010

ISBN 0-7893-0818-5

2002 2003 2004 2005 2006 / 10 9 8 7 6 5 4 3 2 1

Printed and bound in Dubai

Library of Congress Catalog Control Number: 2002108250

Editorial Manager:

Judith More

Art Director:

Penny Stock

Senior Art Editor:

Barbara Zuñiga

Executive Editor:

Zia Mattocks

Design:

LewisHallam

Editors:

Lisa Dyer and Sian Parkhouse

Picture Editor:

Elena Goodinson

Special photography:

Chris Brooks

Production Manager:

Alastair Gourlay

new loft living

Elizabeth Wilhide

Universe

contents

Getting started

Light, airy, open space, flexible planning and multipurpose use: loft living is firmly established as the contemporary ideal. Once a minority enthusiasm of urban adventurers on the cutting edge, today the loft blueprint exerts a powerful influence on the design of our homes, not merely in decoration and materials but also in basic spatial planning.

The development of loft living has been well-charted. But the loft's mutation from avant-garde artist's space to aspirational dream home has also coincided with – if not provoked – an equivalent shift in the way we view our homes and what we now expect them to provide. If loft living is everywhere today – from Manchester to Kansas City, Frankfurt to Toronto – it is because it offers what we increasingly want: free space, light and the opportunity for individual expression.

More than anything else, the arrival of the loft has helped to bring modernity into the mainstream. As a blank canvas, with no conventional domestic markers, the pure space of the loft and the clean lines of modern design have proved an obvious match. Enshrining many of the spatial concepts first put forward by Le Corbusier, Mies van der Rohe and other early modernists over 70 years ago, the loft is a perfect setting for classic contemporary furniture and fittings. At the same time, the loft aesthetic, with its industrial and commercial undertones, has also broadened the decorative vocabulary to the point where it now embraces a host of materials never seen in the domestic arena before, such as stainless steel, glass block and polished concrete. High-tech, the style that was briefly popular around the time the loft movement was just getting underway in the 1970s, was an early manifestation of what has become a defining feature of the modern interior: the use of contrasting surfaces and finishes to create decorative effects that are more than skin deep.

As flexible, adaptable space, the loft also expresses the inclusivity of contemporary living, where activities flow freely from one area to the next. The fluidity and pace of modern society means that traditional domestic planning, where specific activities are assigned separate rooms, no longer feels comfortable or appropriate. We do not want to be confined to the kitchen when friends come to supper and we increasingly work some, or all, of the time from home. The diversity of modern lifestyles means our homes are required to shape-shift, accommodating different activities and different family members at different times. The loft offers the freedom to adapt to changing circumstances, along with a certain liberation from the predictable.

Allied to this freedom of arrangement and function is the scope for individual expression. While many commercially developed loft spaces have displayed a rather bland approach to decoration – the

LEFT **LOFTS OFFER FREEDOM OF EXPRESSION AS WELL AS FLEXIBLE SPATIAL PLANNING. HERE, AN EXPOSED BRICK WALL PROVIDES TEXTURAL DEPTH.**

RIGHT **A CHEAP AND CHEERFUL ECLECTIC MIX OF SALVAGED FITTINGS, TOGETHER WITH A PLAYFUL APPROACH TO DECOR, STRIKES AN ORIGINAL NOTE.**

contemporary cliché of the sweeping expanse of polished wood flooring and pure white plastered (or exposed brick) walls – loft living has always attracted free spirits, eager to give their creative instincts free rein. Salvaged, kitsch or retro elements are as at home in a loft as modern classics and less overpowering than they would be in a more domestically scaled context. Lofts occupy so many types of building, from old spice warehouses and factories to redundant schools and churches, diversity of architectural character is built-in.

Above all, lofts offer spatial quality. Modern life is crowded and stressful; space, for most people, is the ultimate luxury. Even where lofts are not huge cavernous spaces, they still have the potential to create the illusion of spaciousness – often through natural light, height and volume as much as free floor space. It is small wonder that many of the alterations people make to conventional houses and apartments these days result in interior spaces that look more like lofts – in other words, that are open-plan and light-filled.

> Modern life is crowded and
> stressful; space, for most people,
> is the ultimate luxury.

Like any trend that attains the critical mass of widespread popularity and acceptance, loft living has attracted its critics in recent years, a sure sign of its arrival. As the loft aesthetic has developed, much has been made of the distinction between 'true' lofts and 'loft-style' apartments and homes. 'True' lofts, it is often argued, are vast in scale, with the rough industrial edges that betray the rugged non-domestic origins of the buildings in which they are located. On the other hand, 'loft-style' is often denigrated as a convenient tag for what are much more modest, serviced shells. While there is an element of truth in such opinions, the reality is that lofts today come in all shapes and sizes and a host of interior styles, from raw and salvaged to sleek and sophisticated. What makes a loft a loft is no longer simply quantifiable in terms of pedigree or floor area alone, but has to do with more fundamental qualities of planning and design, qualities that are equally applicable in more conventional surroundings. At the turn of the twenty-first century, loft living has truly come of age.

LOFT OPTIONS

During the 1970s, the early days of loft living, you had to be a pretty dedicated and resilient sort of person to live in a loft. Before planning regulations were eased in major cities such as New York and London, permission to convert redundant commercial or industrial premises for residential use was hard to get. Some loft pioneers banded together and bought buildings collectively as a way around this problem; some simply played cat-and-mouse with the authorities, doing their best to conceal the fact that they were living as well as working in the space. Even at their most tolerant, planners tended to insist that former warehouses, factories or offices retained some significant working element, which meant that schemes were only given the go-ahead if you could prove they included studio or workshop facilities.

Early loft living could be hazardous, too. As well as sudden eviction, some loft-dwellers faced the more serious threat of fire. At one time in London's docklands, for example, there was a spate of arson, as warehouse owners discovered that burning down buildings and collecting the insurance money was the most lucrative way of disposing of empty property. Fire was also an ever-present hazard for those who occupied unconverted buildings that were not designed for residential use.

Gradually, however, bureaucracy changed. Authorities became more sympathetic once it was evident that the loft movement was proving a good way of regenerating run-down inner-city areas, and the tide turned away from knocking down old buildings in favour of preserving the urban fabric. In New York, one of the principal centres where the loft movement first got underway, evidence of this shift of opinion came in 1982 with the passing of the 'Loft Law', framed both to ensure that converted buildings were brought up to code for residential use, and hence made safe for their occupants, and to protect the interests of manufacturers who still wanted to maintain premises in the city. As well as bringing much-needed clarity to what had become a free-for-all, legislation paved the way for the

RIGHT LOFTS HAVE INCREASINGLY BECOME THE DEFINING DOMESTIC BLUEPRINT. OPEN-PLAN SPACE OFFERS THE FLEXIBILITY THAT SUITS THE INFORMALITY AND COMPLEXITY OF MODERN LIFESTYLES.

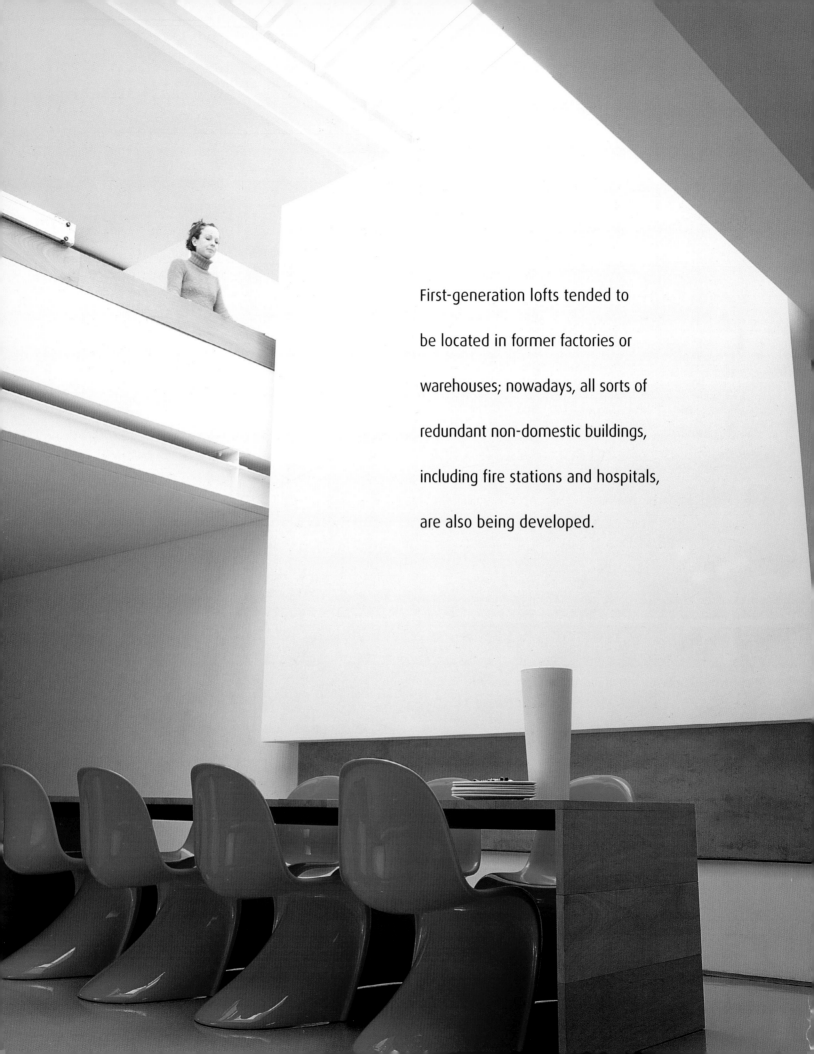

First-generation lofts tended to be located in former factories or warehouses; nowadays, all sorts of redundant non-domestic buildings, including fire stations and hospitals, are also being developed.

creation of new vibrant neighbourhoods that preserved the unique character of the existing factories and warehouses. Arguably, without the loft movement, a great deal of nineteenth-century architectural heritage would have been lost.

Today, while nearly all the hard work has gone out of acquiring a loft, particularly in terms of lengthy wrangles with planning departments, getting the most from loft living can still entail more effort than buying or renting a more conventional home. You may well need the services of an architect or designer to tailor the space to your particular requirements and tastes.

The new emphasis on regeneration means that a much wider scope of buildings is currently being converted into lofts than ever before. First-generation lofts tended to be located in former factories or warehouses; nowadays, all sorts of redundant non-domestic buildings, including fire stations and hospitals, are also being developed. This trend looks set to continue, as the supply of factory and warehouse space dries up and the demand for loft space continues to grow. By the same token, whereas 'loft' was once virtually synonymous with a gritty, downtown location, today loft living can even be found in suburbia, yet more proof of its widespread appeal.

Aside from building type and location, there are a number of other options to consider when choosing a loft, which have implications for budget, potential use and the degree of effort that may be required to adapt the space to your own tastes and requirements. It is important to bear in mind that 'loft' is currently the most overused term in the estate agent's (realtor's) lexicon: make sure you know exactly what you are getting.

FIT-OUTS

Buying or renting a fully fitted loft is exactly the same as buying or renting a house. All the hard work has been done for you. The developer will have acquired the property, obtained the necessary permissions, carried out the basic conversion, added the services

LEFT DRAMATIC SPATIAL VOLUME
AND GREAT NATURAL LIGHT ARE
THE HALLMARKS OF TRUE LOFTS.

and fitted out each loft space with the necessary fixtures, including kitchens, bathrooms and sometimes even flooring.

At the top end of the market, fit-outs can be both innovative and luxurious. Some developments employ name designers and architects as part of the package, which means you can expect a high degree of originality and quality of finish. There may be add-on benefits as well. One recent development of five former factory buildings in London incorporates fully fitted lofts, live–work spaces and offices within the same mixed-use complex, with an on-site café and internet links to generate a community feeling. Another loft development, in the centre of Toronto, provides a basketball court, room service from a restaurant within the building and a rooftop terrace where you can walk your dog.

At the lower end of the fit-out market, however, you may find that the space has been designed and finished with an eye for economy, which may mean you would be better opting for a shell space instead.

SHELL SPACES

Many of the lofts that come onto the market are shell spaces. As in the case of fit-outs, the really difficult issues of structural conversion, servicing and permissions will already have been tackled by the building's developer. Some shell spaces are precisely that and require everything from heating systems to kitchens and bathrooms. Others are minimally fitted; some may feature new mezzanine levels or other structural features that the builder or developer has added as a selling point. Again, the quality and size of the space varies with price – many shell spaces at the bottom end of the market, where a developer may have tried to carve up a building into as many units as possible, lack both character and floor area and are essentially little more than starter homes with an upmarket name.

Shell spaces are popular because they allow you to tap into the original pioneering spirit of the loft movement and configure the space any way you choose. The downside is that you need to budget and plan carefully and specialist help is almost always a good idea, if only to ensure that what you are planning to do is legal and achievable. Mortgage lenders are also reluctant to advance more than 80 per cent of the cost of a shell, which means you will have to put more money up front. In terms of fitting out, you need to set a realistic budget and stick to it. Costs can add up, so you must have a clear idea from the outset of how much you can afford to spend on the space and what this is likely to get.

If your shell is completely unfitted, you will almost certainly need to employ an architect. He or she will not only be able to envision different layouts and spatial arrangements, but will also ensure that any structural work, such as adding a new mezzanine level, for example, is safe and legal, and will make sure that the fitted shell meets all fire and building regulations. You may also need to consult other experts, too. Open spaces, particularly those that are double-height, are notoriously difficult to heat and you may need the advice of a plumbing contractor or heating engineer to establish the right number and positioning of radiators.

Some developers can recommend architects, designers or builders to carry out the work for you. Before you choose, look at their portfolios to see if the type of work they do appeals. A good match between client and designer is the basis of every successful scheme.

LIVE–WORK

In the days when planners were reluctant to award 'change of use' to a property, a prerequisite of gaining permission to convert a commercial building into a residence was to retain at least some working element on site, such as a workshop or photographer's studio. The guidelines have now changed and many loft spaces are available specifically as 'live–work' units. Some are equipped fully wired for internet and high-tech communication.

If one of your reasons for loft living in the first place is to work from home, choosing a live–work unit can be a sensible option. Because working from home means no commuting and more flexibility, it is an increasingly attractive career move. However, there are also financial and legal implications, and it is advisable to check these out in detail before you proceed. In Britain, for example, regulations specify how much of the overall space can be used for working – generally between 30 and 50 per cent – and the type of business allowed. You can run an office or a studio from a live–work unit, provided the work does not adversely affect neighbours in terms

of noise, pollution, traffic or other environmental considerations; there may be restrictions on signage, too, and visitors to your business must be by appointment only. On the financial side, owners or tenants of live–work units generally pay a combination of business and local rates, but are allowed to offset a proportion of household expenses against tax. If you are self-employed, desk-bound and neither clients nor suppliers visit on a regular basis, there may be no particular advantage in a live–work unit.

DO-IT-YOURSELF

In the beginning, all lofts by their very nature were do-it-yourself. While planners are much more sympathetic to such schemes than they were even ten years ago, finding a derelict or redundant building and raising the necessary finance for its purchase and wholesale structural conversion is no easier for the private individual nowadays and may even be harder, given the competition from large developers and builders who have moved into this market sector with a vengeance. Planning is still an issue, however, and some authorities will not grant 'change of use' until the building has been converted, a risk not everyone is prepared to take. On the finance side, one option is to form an association with others interested in loft living and to pool resources; in which case, legal advice should be taken and an agreement drawn up between all parties to prevent future disputes.

Today, with so many shells on the market, there are less obvious advantages to do-it-yourself, but it can still be tempting, particularly if you spot an idiosyncratic or beautiful building that the market has overlooked. Smaller properties or those in difficult locations (beside a railway line, for example) offer the most potential for private development, since there will be less competition. However, many seemingly abandoned or derelict buildings have complicated histories and thorough research will be required to uncover all the relevant issues prior to purchase – access and servicing can be especially problematic. Similarly, in-depth structural surveys should be commissioned to determine the physical condition of the building so you know exactly what you are letting yourself in for.

RIGHT A BEAUTIFULLY DETAILED OPEN STAIRCASE WITH WOODEN TREADS LEADS TO A MEZZANINE LEVEL. IT IS NEATLY FITTED WITH STORAGE UNDERNEATH, CLEVERLY CONCEALED BEHIND FLUSH PANELS.

CHOOSING A LOFT

While most of us know what to look for when buying a house
or apartment and are aware of the common pitfalls, lofts are
a relatively recent phenomenon and you will need to exercise
greater care before signing on the dotted line.

· Consult specialists who have experience in loft development.
  This includes mortgage lenders and brokers and lawyers,
  as well as architects and designers.

· Big spaces with large windows are very seductive. But think
  about what it will be like to live in the space. Will it be difficult

to heat or cool? How much privacy is there? Is it noisy? How readily can storage space be built in?

- If you haven't lived in a loft before, it is likely that at least some of the furniture you own will not look right in the space. You should add in the cost of replacing furniture to the other costs associated with buying, renting or fitting out.

- Make sure you know exactly what you are getting. Scrutinize the fine print in brochures, particularly if the developer is offering a fit-out to your specification. If the development includes special amenities, there may be associated maintenance costs, for example.

- Opt for lofts that have been developed by companies with a good track record. Inspect the property thoroughly to make sure fittings, fixtures and finishes are high quality.

- If you are buying a shell, expect to pay a substantial proportion of the purchase price to fit it out. And expect the work to take time.

1 space planning

Loft living is all about space. Massive floor area, big windows and high ceilings are naturally uplifting and exhilarating in comparison to more conventionally scaled interiors – and such features make compelling selling points when so much of modern life can be cramped and stressful. But just as important as size and scale is the disposition of space. Loft living, with its flow of free space and flexible divisions, signals a whole new attitude to the way a home is planned and used.

Traditional homes, subdivided into rooms nominally assigned specific functions, reflect a way of life increasingly at odds with current social trends. Separate rooms on different levels require stairs, landings, halls and corridors to connect them so a large amount of floor area in a conventionally arranged home is taken up by such circulation space. The loft movement has revealed the many ways in which ordinary homes no longer fit our lifestyles. But free space does not guarantee spatial quality. Few people are at ease living in the indoor equivalent of a football field; there needs to be a balance between openness and enclosure. And spatial quality is further enhanced by exploiting the rhythms of light and shade to make an environment that is as natural and comfortable as possible.

Assessment

A blank sheet can be daunting and in spatial terms a loft represents the blankest sheet of all. An essential starting point is assessing your requirements and the qualities of the space itself. The more specific you can be, the better and more successful the final result will be.

Most people are attracted to loft living because it offers spatial freedom, along with robust architectural character. Space is all very well, but you have to fit your life into it somehow. To begin, note the features you would preserve at any cost, such as exposed architecture; large windows or skylights; original surfaces; or simply the feeling of openness. Next, consider your patterns of living. Think about the following questions, as they can steer you in a specific direction, or form the basis of the design brief to an architect.

PREVIOUS PAGE DECIDING WHERE TO LOCATE THE KITCHEN AND HOW MUCH SPACE TO DEVOTE TO IT CAN HELP TO SET PARAMETERS WHEN IT COMES TO PLANNING A LOFT. IF YOU LIKE COOKING AND ENTERTAIN OFTEN, A COOKING AREA CAN BE PROMINENT.

BELOW A GRAND PIANO TAKES PRIDE OF PLACE IN THE CENTRAL HALLWAY THAT LEADS FROM THE LIVING AREA TO THE STUDY AND BETWEEN THE BEDROOM AND KITCHEN OF THIS MANHATTAN LOFT – A SPATIAL LUXURY FEW CAN AFFORD.

ASSESSING YOUR NEEDS

- **How you prepare food should determine how much space you allocate to a kitchen area and where it is located. Are you an enthusiastic cook who likes to entertain or a social butterfly who can just about manage to boil a kettle? If cooking is a big part of your life, you might want the kitchen area to take centre stage in the main space. But if you cook infrequently and reluctantly, a minimal kitchen, fitted as part of a storage wall so that it folds away when not in use, can be an ideal solution.**

- **Do you prefer showers to baths, or want both? Showers are obviously more space-saving, but bathtubs can also be located within sleeping areas if privacy is not an important issue.**

- **How much storage do you need? Assessing storage requirements should not be done on the basis of optimistic guesswork. You will only determine how much space you need to house your clothes, books, CDs, files and other possessions if you get out your measuring tape. Nothing compromises a sense of space more than clutter, which generally means that discreet storage for at least some of your belongings is a good idea. However, for concealed storage to work, dimensions must be planned according to the number, size and shape of what you intend to store, allowing a generous margin for future acquisitions.**

- **Do you need a dedicated workspace? Does your work require natural light, peace and quiet or special equipment? Do you prefer to screen your work from view or are you comfortable leaving it out in the open?**

- **How many bedrooms or sleeping areas do you need? Do you often have guests to stay? Is it important to be able to enclose a sleeping area all or part of the time?**

- **Have you any possessions which you must find room for, such as a piano, a collection of pictures or a treasured antique?**

STRUCTURAL FEATURES, SUCH
AS THESE CAST-IRON COLUMNS,
MAY SET LIMITS ON HOW YOU
SUBDIVIDE SPACE. THIS OPEN
KITCHEN IS ALIGNED ALONG
ONE WALL, SEPARATED FROM THE
MAIN SPACE BY A ISLAND COUNTER.

Specialist help

Before you start mentally hanging pictures and arranging furniture, it is important to identify what specialist support you are going to need. A great deal will depend on the extent to which your loft is already serviced and how much scope it provides for alternative layouts. If the basics are in place, you may find that you need only employ builders, carpenters or specialist subcontractors such as floor-layers on a job-by-job basis. That way you can tackle different areas or elements over time, which will enable you to fund the work in stages. The same applies if your loft is on the small side and there is only one sensible way of configuring the space. Beware, however, of taking on more than you can realistically cope with. If you are having a lot of work done, you will need to be sure that everything happens in the correct sequence, which will mean chasing up suppliers, organizing deliveries and booking in subcontractors at the appropriate times. If you don't think you can take the pressure – or the time off work – get an architect, interior designer or builder to project-manage the scheme for you.

ARCHITECTS AND INTERIOR DESIGNERS

There are specific circumstances in which you will need to employ an architect. This will be the case if your loft is a true shell, with connections to services but nothing else, or if you want to make significant structural alterations or change existing fittings in a radical manner – moving the location of a kitchen, for example. The same applies if your loft is big and has the potential for different spatial arrangements. Big lofts with high ceilings offer the opportunity to exploit volume, and thinking about space in terms of volume is something few nonprofessionals are able to do (see pages 40–43).

Architects combine design flair with practical expertise to ensure that work proceeds to budget and on time and that the final result complies fully with current regulations – an important and often-overlooked point. You can either employ them solely to interpret your ideas and come up with a number of possible solutions, or you can ask them to oversee the whole project from start to finish, and liaise with builders, suppliers and subcontractors until the work is completed to everyone's satisfaction.

Architects are often misrepresented as domineering characters who bulldoze clients into schemes they neither like nor can afford. When that happens the problem can usually be traced to a poor match of client and professional. For example, don't hire a minimalist if your taste tends toward the baroque. Do your research; find an architect who has designed the sort of spaces you would like to live in.

> If you don't think you can take the pressure, get an architect, interior designer or builder to project-manage the scheme for you.

As is the case when employing any professional, be absolutely clear what you want and what you are getting. A written brief is a good starting point. Don't be vague about how much you can spend and make sure you get a realistic idea about how long the work should take. Finally, try to resist the temptation to change your mind halfway through – there's no better way of ending up vastly overbudget and weeks behind schedule.

If you are short on ideas and are looking for originality and a high standard of finish, you may want to seek out the services of an interior designer. Interior designers are not qualified to advise on structural matters or building regulations, but they can tackle spatial planning, kitchen and bathroom design, and come up with innovative schemes for lighting, fittings and furnishings. Employing an interior designer makes sense if your loft requires no major alterations and you're after something a little different.

RULES AND REGULATIONS

Like any other residential property, a loft must comply with a number of rules and regulations, chiefly designed to ensure your health and safety and that of your neighbours, and to maintain overall structural integrity. These regulations vary from area to area and from country

to country, and are often updated and changed. If you're planning major alterations, you'll need expert advice from the outset, preferably from an architect, to help negotiate the bureaucratic hurdles.

While most of the codes governing the use and alteration of residential buildings are founded in straightforward common sense, you may well find that some of the finer points can rule out more elegant design solutions. At times this can be so frustrating that it can be tempting to proceed without the necessary permissions. Bear in mind, however, that unless your loft is fully code-compliant or has received a building inspector's certificate, it will be illegal and you may face further action. It may also be difficult to sell in the future.

Local planning laws govern the changes that are permitted to the external appearance of the building, extensions, change of use and issues relating to neighbouring properties, particularly in respect to natural light. If you are buying a loft within a development, you are unlikely to need further planning permissions. But if your loft is on the top floor and you plan changes that will affect the shape of the roof, planning permission will probably be required. New consent will also be needed if you plan to subdivide your loft in such a way as to exceed the quota of 'habitable rooms'. A 'habitable room' is any fully self-contained area that is not a kitchen, bathroom, hallway or landing. All habitable rooms must have at least one window and the number allowed for each loft will have been set as part of the original planning permission for the conversion of the building.

Building regulations approval is also required if you make any structural changes. Examples include adding a mezzanine level, changing the location of a staircase, cutting away part of an existing floor, making new openings in external walls or enlarging existing openings, and making new openings in load-bearing internal walls. Other regulations regarding safety, drainage and fire protection may also affect design and choice of materials – everything from the siting of power points to the detailing of staircases.

LEFT A DRAMATIC MEZZANINE SERVES AS STUDY AND LIBRARY. SUSPENDED FROM THE ROOF, IT IS ACCESSED BY A NARROW FLIGHT OF OPEN STAIRS.

PROFESSIONAL DESIGNERS WILL NOT ONLY ENSURE SUCH ADDITIONS ARE SOUND BUT WILL BE ABLE TO COME UP WITH ORIGINAL SOLUTIONS.

Servicing

DESIGNING SERVICING

· **Build in flexibility. Make sure that there are enough power points, especially in kitchen, living and working areas where the demand will be greatest . The more power points there are, the easier it will be to alter the way you use the space in the future if you need to.**

· **Think high-tech. Install the latest lines of communication and consider programmable lighting, security and music systems. Centralized controls of such systems are ideal for one-space living and help to integrate different areas. It is far less disruptive to install the necessary cabling and outlets before you have decorated or brought in furniture.**

· **Open kitchen areas must be fitted with a good mechanical extractor: cooking smells are appetizing; stale cooking smells are not. You will also need mechanical ventilation if a bathroom has no window.**

· **If there is a potential noise problem, you may need to install acoustic insulation within floors or walls.**

· **Big windows can drain heat from the interior during the winter and cause overheating in summer. Consider replacing standard glass with low-E glazing (low-emissivity, high-performance insulating glass), or double- or triple-glazed units for better insulation. These types of glazing are quite expensive, but the costs will be offset against lower heating and cooling bills.**

· **Seek advice when it comes to choosing a heating system and positioning heat outlets or radiators. Low-level or vertical radiators are less intrusive in an open space than conventional radiators and keep wall space free. Underfloor heating, although it is more expensive, can be a very effective way of heating a loft, particularly when it is used in combination with hard flooring, such as concrete or stone, materials that retain heat longer.**

When it comes to spatial planning, the servicing – water and gas pipes and outlets, and electricity, telephone and high-tech cabling – sets certain parameters that limit your choices. But at the same time, lofts by their very nature offer the opportunity to configure service areas in a freer and more dynamic way.

In conventional homes arranged over two or more storeys, there's always that feeling that the bathroom is bound to be 'first on the right at the top of the stairs'. Making changes to servicing in these homes can often be extremely disruptive and expensive, which tends to put people off radical alterations. A loft, on the other hand, particularly a shell, allows more flexibility when deciding on the location of kitchens, bathrooms and other service areas. Starting with these functional elements often results in more workable space all-round. Developers are aware that freedom of choice is a selling point and many serviced shells offer a choice of servicing points.

For reasons of economy and simplicity, it makes sense to unite kitchen and bathroom areas within a single serviced core, either grouped centrally or stacked one on top of the other. In fact, the central service core has become a specific feature of loft design. It expresses a robust and functional approach that is in keeping with the overall aesthetic and makes areas that have traditionally been kept out of the main view prominent.

Open-plan kitchen areas or kitchens located in the heart of a living space have lost their shock appeal, although it was not that long ago when such an approach was radical in the extreme. Now, however, the boundaries are also breaking down from around that most private of all domestic retreats, the bathroom. This trend has manifested itself in a number of ways. One is the sudden surge in popularity of wet rooms. With all surfaces fully waterproof and showers draining directly into the floor, wet rooms take the 'room' out of 'bathroom'. Sleek and unencumbered by conventional fittings, wet rooms need not be fully enclosed but can be screened from other areas by simple curving partitions or by high-tech glass panels that turn from transparent to opaque at the flick of a switch. Another

manifestation of open bathing is where bathtubs are sited within a bedroom or sleeping space, acknowledging the fundamental connection between relaxing, resting and soaking in the bath. While toilets have yet to come out of the closet there's evidence of a new boldness in this area, too, with new designs housed in pods or capsules right in the main space, rather like those futuristic street conveniences. In one London loft, a toilet and sink are enclosed by curving walls of opaque frosted glass, dramatically lit from within.

ABOVE AN ISLAND COUNTER DOUBLES UP AS A BREAKFAST BAR AND SCREENS VIEWS OF WORKSURFACES AND APPLIANCES FROM THE MAIN SPACE.

RIGHT SITE LIVING AND RELAXING AREAS WHERE THE QUALITY OF NATURAL LIGHT IS OPTIMUM. HERE, WALL-HUNG RADIATORS MAXIMIZE AVAILABLE WALL SPACE.

One-space living

If open space is what has attracted you to loft living in the first place, the last thing you will want to do is break it up into individual rooms. But at the same time, it can be both uncomfortable and impractical to live your entire life out in the open. On the practical side, open space can be noisy and hard to heat; on the psychological level, there are times at which full exposure feels threatening rather than uplifting. Many loft enthusiasts who initially opt for a fully open arrangement find themselves putting up a few walls at a later date. Although many loft shells converted from twentieth-century buildings are entirely open, lofts in older buildings may feature supporting columns or piers, and these structural elements may dictate how you can subdivide the space.

While getting the balance right between openness and enclosure is very much a personal issue, it can be useful to divide activities – and hence areas within the space – into public and private. This does not entail a retreat into the convention of separate rooms, but brackets those activities together which have most in common. Overlapping sociable activities, such as relaxing, eating and cooking, keeps lines of communication open and promotes a sense of informality. Sleeping and bathing, on the other hand, are activities where we feel more vulnerable, and can usefully be combined in a more enclosed area.

When loft-livers find themselves putting up walls, in most cases it is to enclose a sleeping area. 'Nesting' is a strong human instinct and it simply feels more natural and comfortable to have the protective security of walls around you when you are sleeping. Separating sleeping areas from the rest of the household prevents

RIGHT IN THIS OPEN-PLAN LOFT, ALTHOUGH ALL AREAS REMAIN ON VIEW, THERE IS A CLEAR DISTINCTION BETWEEN DIFFERENT TYPES OF ACTIVITY. THE CENTRAL KITCHEN SEPARATES AN EATING AREA IN THE FOREGROUND FROM THE LIVING AREA OCCUPYING ONE ARM OF THE L-SHAPED LAYOUT. FLOORING IS A UNIFYING FEATURE.

the awkwardness of sharing intimate moments with guests and/or children. If the sleeping area also includes a tub for bathing, you can retain an element of the freedom that a fully open space provides.

It's not just what you enclose,

it's how you enclose it.

In general, it is best to allocate most space, in floor area and volume, to the sociable activities of relaxing, eating and cooking. These functions also benefit from optimal natural light. But sleeping areas need not be extensive, nor particularly well-lit, since they are chiefly used at night. Habitable rooms, which include bedrooms, must have at least one window, so your options may be more limited, particularly if your loft is single-aspect.

It's not just what you enclose, it's how you enclose it. There's no need to opt for the conventional domestic blueprint of straight walls, regular-shaped and sized rooms and standard-door heights when it

comes to dividing space; more creative and unusual alternatives do the job just as well but maintain that essential loft aesthetic and overall feeling of spaciousness.

WALLS AND PARTITIONS

Curved, snaking or angled walls dispel any hint of boxiness. A curved wall is particularly effective if you are enclosing a shower or wet room behind it, and it has a pleasing sculptural quality that adds character and a certain dynamic to a space. However, curves are harder to construct than straight lines and generally cost more.

Half-height or half-width partitions are another possibility. Whereas these sort of enclosures do not provide the degree of separation you may require for a sleeping area, they can usefully define a kitchen from a main living space, or a bathing area from a sleeping area, without blocking light or views. A half-height partition-cum-counter that marks the extent of a kitchen will screen some of the activity and clutter of preparation from view – which can be particularly welcome if you are a diffident cook – while still retaining the feeling of openness. A panel-like partition in a combined sleeping and washing area can serve as a headboard on one side and be fitted with sinks, showers or a tub on the other.

When enclosing areas with fixed or built-in space dividers, it is a good idea to experiment with unconventional materials rather than simply default to plain plastered walls. Translucent materials, such as glass block or frosted and laminated glass, allow light to filter through. Concrete can be highly effective; whether polished smooth or finished with a suede-like texture, its monumental quality works well with the scale and character of a loft. The shimmering surface of mosaic accentuates curved partitions, but even simply painting a divider a strong colour will make the whole effect look well-considered.

ENTRANCES AND OPENINGS

Flexible, sliding or folding partitions are where walls meet doors. These largely bespoke elements can be arranged, fitted and detailed in a variety of ways; they can be pivoted, top-hung or run along floor tracks to screen or open out space as required. In many cases, these movable walls consist of a relatively light or translucent material, such as glass, Perspex or metal mesh, framed in metal or wood.

As far as exits and entrances are concerned, there is no reason why you should adhere to standard door heights, even where the space is enclosed with solid floor-to-ceiling walls. Dispensing with the door head – the portion of wall above the door – so that the opening extends right up to the ceiling, means that both the enclosed area and the adjoining space will read as a whole when the door is open, because the ceiling and floor planes are uninterrupted. In this case, opting for a sliding panel or a panel that retracts within the door opening, rather than a door that opens on hinges, will accentuate the effect further.

OPPOSITE ONE WAY OF RINGING THE CHANGES WHEN IT COMES TO ADDING PARTITIONS OR SPATIAL DIVIDERS IS TO USE UNCONVENTIONAL MATERIALS, SUCH AS GLASS BRICK.

BELOW PIVOTING FLOOR-TO-CEILING PARTITIONS INFILLED WITH OPAQUE GLASS PROVIDE FLEXIBLE SPATIAL DIVIDERS WITHOUT CREATING THE EFFECT OF INDIVIDUAL 'ROOMS'.

MOVABLE DIVIDERS

If you are renting a loft, are limited by a tight budget or are simply uncertain as to how to subdivide the space, cheaper and less permanent solutions include using curtains (drapes), blinds (shades), screens or large pieces of furniture to demarcate different areas.

Curtains and blinds do not block much in the way of noise, but they can make simple and effective ways of screening off sleeping areas, work stations or storage, providing some privacy and hiding clutter from general view. Soft furnishings inevitably have rather traditional associations, so it is best to banish any conventional overtones by opting for unusual materials and simple, robust treatments. Soft folds of brightly coloured felt, filmy white translucent drapery hung along ceiling tracks, sailcloth laced to metal poles, metal mesh, PVC and plastic and bold contemporary or exotic printed textiles can all have

an appropriately theatrical impact. Roller, Venetian or slatted wooden blinds (shades) work well as flexible dividers, or hung against internal glass partitions to screen views.

More minimally, a mere suggestion of separation can be achieved by using screens. Screens are mobile punctuation points, good for adding a little privacy or signalling a change of activity. There are a wide variety of contemporary screens on the market in a range of sizes and in materials from plywood to Perspex, but you can also

BELOW **MAKING AN ATTRACTIVE FEATURE OF THE NEED FOR ENCLOSURE, THIS FREESTANDING PLYWOOD BOX HOUSES A LAVATORY AND WASHBASIN.**

RIGHT **AN INGENIOUS SLEEPING POD FOR A YOUNG CHILD, THIS MODULE IS MADE FROM CURVED SECTIONS OF RECLAIMED PLYWOOD AND SCREENED BY A CURTAIN.**

customize commercial screens (the sort used to break up the space in open-plan office layouts) with any material of choice or have a screen made up to your dimensions and specification.

Furniture also has a role to play when it comes to defining different areas. It is important to get the 'skyline' right. An open space filled with groups of furniture of similar height can resemble a furniture warehouse. Better definition can be achieved with freestanding storage units or room dividers that break up the horizon.

MODULES AND PODS

Hiving off activities into self-contained modules or pods is just one of the many ways the loft has redefined how we think about space. Less a room within a room and more capsule or cockpit, the pod is a compact and often mobile solution. It is being increasingly adopted by loft-livers as a way of creating an enclosed space for sleeping, working or even entertainment. Pods or modules allow you to keep the rest of the space free and unfettered, while providing a personal enclave that does not commit you to a more

permanent spatial arrangement. Freewheeling pods and modules always work best, however, where there is plenty of free space surrounding them and a good ceiling height. They can look clumsy and are not particularly effective in smaller lofts.

An early manifestation of this idea was Douglas Ball's Clipper CS-1 workstation, designed in 1994 to aid concentrated work in an open-plan office. It is a friendly, organically shaped capsule with blinds (shades) and a flap-down work surface. Similar ideas have surfaced in the form of salvaged oil tanks or cement mixers, used as sleeping capsules. Many mobile modules serve as children's rooms and offer just the sort of den-like playful space children love.

FLOORING

If you don't want any degree of separation, a simple shift of flooring material or a step up or down can signpost a change of area or activity. A kitchen area raised on a shallow platform defines itself within an open space, while floorboards giving way to soft carpet announces a move from living areas to a sleeping space.

case study

The term 'loft' may be bandied about somewhat indiscriminately these days, but this particular example has all the right credentials. To begin with, there's the authentic location, a gritty inner-city area near a mainline station; then the size, a very generous 207 sq m (2,230 sq ft); and, finally, the industrial pedigree: the building was once both a feather warehouse and a factory where paper poppies were made to commemorate the war dead on Remembrance (Memorial) Day. The huge amount of floor area alone would qualify it as most people's idea of an urban dream home.

Yet, like many true lofts, this one had its attendant disadvantages. One-space living tends not to be too much of an adjustment for a single person, but for couples, and especially families, issues such as privacy, sound levels and spatial definition assume much more importance.

When the loft was acquired by a couple with two young children, it was simply a vast rectangular shell, with a wall of floor-to-ceiling windows overlooking a busy publishing office. There was no privacy (the offices are occupied day and night) and the open, undefined space was not so much exhilarating as intimidating and at the same time rather bland and featureless. The challenge was to create a comfortable family home without losing spatial quality or adopting the rather clinical and unimaginative style of the typical developer's choice of fixtures.

A number of different strategies were employed to create distinct areas within the space. A key decision was to break up the basic rectangle with two semi-circular shapes: one open, housing the kitchen; and one closed, providing privacy for the bathroom and defining the more private areas at the rear of the loft where

the two bedrooms are located. In the main open-plan area, this organic curve is further emphasized by changes in floor level, which create platforms at different levels. The living and dining areas are on one level, while the children's play area is a step above.

A loft provides the opportunity to divide space without recourse to conventional rectilinear walls and doors. The curved wall that encloses the bathroom is infilled with a strip of translucent glass bricks to keep a light and airy feel. In the corridor outside the bathroom is a pair of pivoting custom-designed screens on castors that can be swung across to close off the bedroom area from the main circulation routes. Made of brushed steel and beech, the screens are curved in section, an obvious reference to aeronautical design. Added to which, movable wrought-iron screens, large plants and shelving units serve as

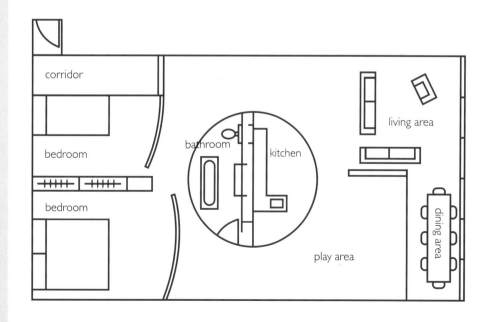

LEFT: THE FLOOR PLAN OF THE LOFT REVEALS THE CENTRAL SEMI-CIRCLES, ONE OF WHICH DEFINES THE KITCHEN AND THE OTHER HOUSES THE BATHROOM. THE PIVOTING CURVED SCREENS PROVIDE FLEXIBLE SPACE DIVIDERS.

RIGHT: IN THIS VIEW OF THE MAIN LIVING/ DINING SPACE A SEATING AREA IS RAISED UP ON A PLATFORM; TOWARDS THE REAR OF THE SPACE A CHILDREN'S PLAY AREA IS SET ON A LEVEL ABOVE. A BOOKCASE ON CASTORS, WROUGHT-IRON SCREENS AND A LARGE PLANT DIVIDE THE SPACE INFORMALLY.

informal punctuation points in the main space. The result retains all the benefits of one-space open-plan living with none of the drawbacks, and without resorting to standard, boxy partitions.

Complementing this relaxed, workable layout is a palette of warm, contrasting materials. The main floor is reclaimed pitch pine from an architectural salvage company; the bathroom flooring is green slate. The door to the hallway is covered with patinated copper, while the overscaled master bed is made of untreated wood. Furnishings and fixtures are an eclectic mixture of designer and retro, with antique kelims and Indian wall-hangings adding a sense of comfort and character.

OPPOSITE ABOVE: THE WIDE CIRCULAR SWEEP OF THE RAISED WOODEN PLATFORM CLEARLY DELINEATES THE KITCHEN AREA WITHIN THE OPEN-PLAN LIVING SPACE. THE USE OF WARM MATERIALS, SUCH AS RICHLY COLOURED RECLAIMED PINE BOARDS AND THE EXPOSED BRICK WALLS, PROVIDES FURTHER VISUAL TEXTURE AND DEPTH OF CHARACTER.

OPPOSITE BELOW: THIS VIEW OF THE MAIN SPACE IS LOOKING IN THE OPPOSITE DIRECTION FROM THE RAISED PLAY AREA. THE VARIOUS FUNCTIONAL AREAS WITHIN THE SPACE ARE DEFINED WITHOUT COMPROMISING THE ABUNDANT FEELING OF SPACE. GARLANDS OF HOPS FESTOON THE KITCHEN WALL. PENDANT INDUSTRIAL-STYLE GALVANIZED STEEL FITTINGS LIGHT THE KITCHEN AREA.

ABOVE LEFT: THE CORRIDOR OUTSIDE THE BATHROOM LEADS TOWARDS THE REAR OF THE LOFT WHERE THE BEDROOMS ARE LOCATED. THE USE OF CURVED PARTITIONS RATHER THAN STRAIGHT WALLS MAINTAINS THE FEELING OF A FLUID TRANSITION BETWEEN AREAS.

ABOVE RIGHT: THE SEMI-CIRCULAR BATHROOM WALL IS INFILLED WITH GLASS BRICKS FOR EXTRA LIGHT. FLOORING IS GREEN SLATE. THE FREESTANDING CLAW-FOOT BATHTUB TAKES CENTRE STAGE IN THE GENEROUS SPACE.

case study

Located in a former frame factory in the centre of Ghent, Belgium, in a 1920s building, this top-floor loft combines a rugged industrial backdrop with finely detailed new surfaces and finishes. The architect and owner of the loft had been looking for a building which had some of the gritty atmosphere of lofts in the industrial areas of big metropolitan centres, such as New York and London. What convinced him about this space was both its relative seclusion, tucked away in a densely populated area, and the expansive view over the surrounding city. From the street, all that is visible is the main entrance; once inside the top level of the three-storey building there is a feeling of having arrived at a private island.

Although the original structure was sound, all the servicing needed to be installed, including an industrial heating system. The top floor became a home for the architect and his family (which includes two small children); the remaining floors house a carport, storage area and two smaller lofts.

The main concept with regard to the spatial planning was to retain the open quality of a loft and avoid creating simply a big apartment. At the same time, a fully open layout would not have provided the necessary privacy and separation of activities that families with small children require. To this end, the more private spaces – bedrooms, bathroom and dressing area – are grouped along one side, with openings in between so that the old walls of the original structure can be seen from each individual area. The flexibility of this layout results in a dynamic circulation pattern, providing different options for getting from one part of the loft to another – a feature in which the children and their friends take considerable delight.

LEFT: THE KITCHEN ISLAND, MADE OF BLUESTONE AND DESIGNED BY THE ARCHITECT-OWNER, OCCUPIES A CENTRAL POSITION IN THE MAIN SPACE OF THE LOFT, REFLECTING THE FAMILY'S LOVE OF COOKING AND ENTERTAINING. LIGHT FITTINGS THROUGHOUT WERE ALSO DESIGNED BY THE OWNER, INCLUDING SPECIAL ULTRA-VIOLET STRIP LIGHTS WHICH ACCENTUATE SPATIAL VOLUME BY NIGHT.

RIGHT: A VIEW OF THE MAIN OPEN SPACE OF THE LOFT SHOWS THE DINING TABLE CENTRALLY POSITIONED UNDER TWO SKYLIGHTS. THE FLOORING IN THIS PART IS THE ORIGINAL CONCRETE. A CEDAR-CLAD PARTITION ANNOUNCES THE TRANSITION TO THE MORE PRIVATE AREAS AND SCREENS THE VIEW OF THE BATHROOM.

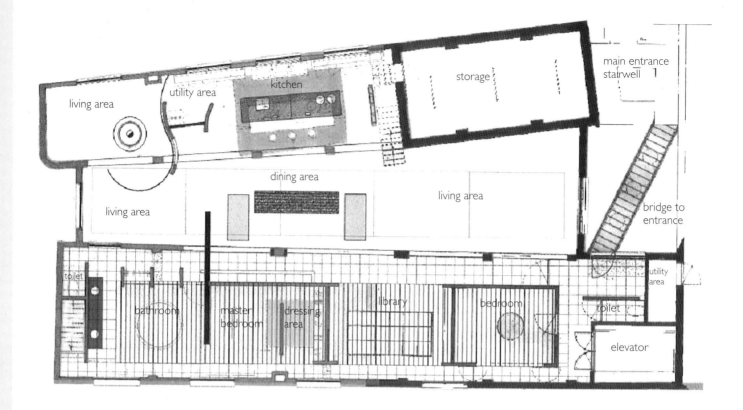

living area

utility area

kitchen

storage

main entrance stairwell

dining area

living area

living area

bridge to entrance

toilet

bathroom

master bedroom

dressing area

library

bedroom

toilet

utility area

elevator

ABOVE: THE LOFT IS LAID OUT WITH AN OPEN FLEXIBLE MULTIPURPOSE AREA TO ONE SIDE OF THE LOFT AND MORE PRIVATE SPACES ON THE OTHER. IN THE PRIVATE AREA, FLOORING IS A MIXTURE OF NATURAL STONE AND PARQUET.

RIGHT: THE PARTITIONS WHICH SUBDIVIDE SPACE IN THE PRIVATE ZONE STOP SHORT OF THE ORIGINAL BRICK WALLS OF THE LOFT, SO THAT THESE SUBDIVIDED AREAS STILL FEEL LIKE PART OF THE MAIN SPACE AND NOT SELF-CONTAINED ROOMS.

FAR RIGHT: FOUR METAL BATHROOM CABINETS HUNG IN THE SHAPE OF A CROSS PROVIDE AN ORIGINAL TAKE ON BATHROOM STORAGE.

OVERLEAF: A VIEW THROUGH THE 'PRIVATE' ZONE SHOWS THE SPATIAL PARTITIONS AND THE SHIFT OF FLOORING MATERIAL. THE BATHROOM PARTITION IS CLAD IN AROMATIC CEDAR.

case study

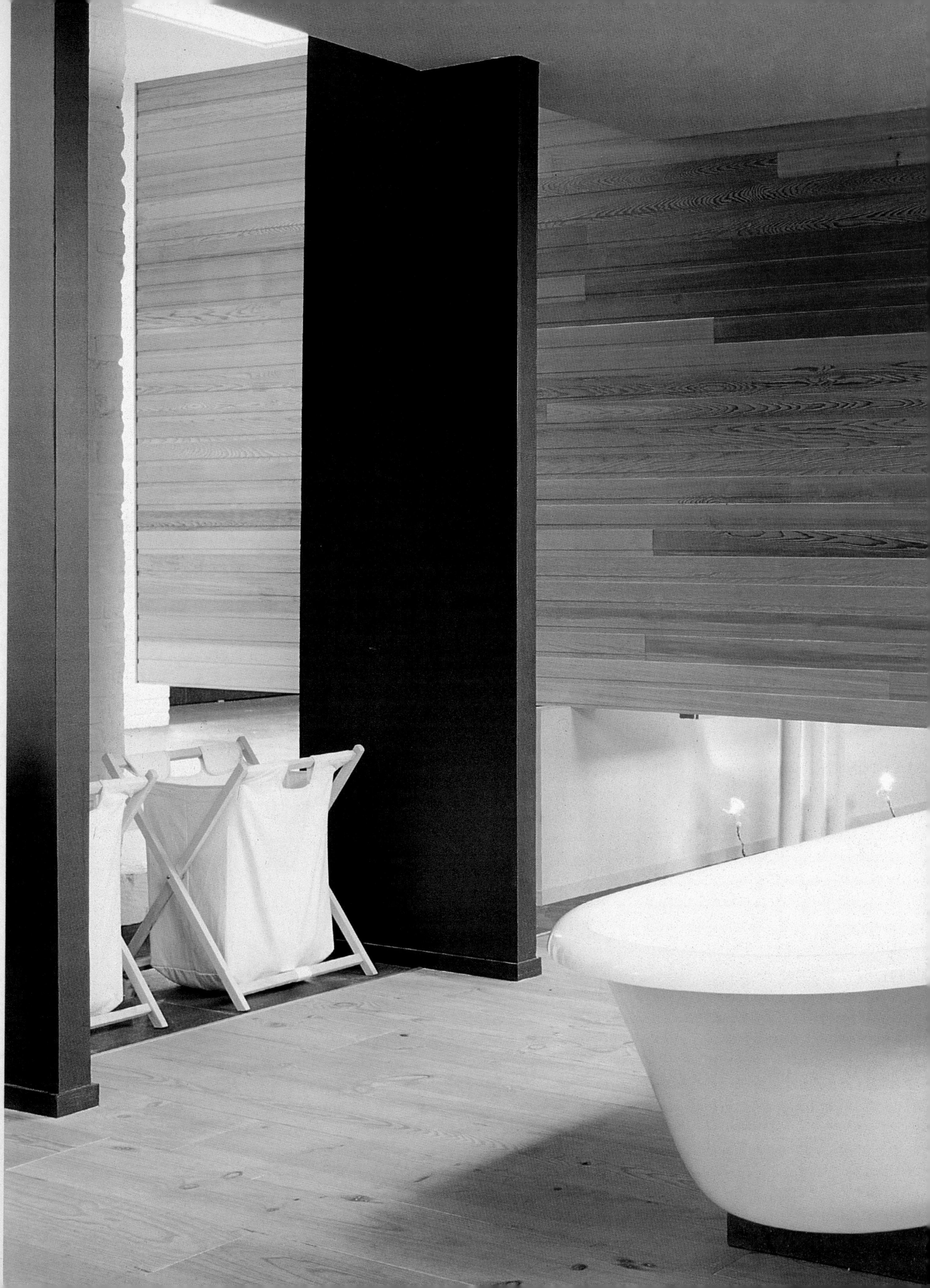

Volume

Loft living requires that you think three-dimensionally, in terms of volume as much as floor area. Most people assess space by area alone, which makes sense in a standard interior with little variation in ceiling height. True lofts, however, often have very high ceilings, which brings the issue of volume into sharper focus. Where a loft occupies an upper storey of an older building, the roof structure may be exposed, which adds another dynamic. High-ceilinged spaces mean you can introduce galleries and mezzanine levels, increasing the floor area without losing the overall feeling of spaciousness. Although double-height spaces offer the greatest potential in this respect, a loft with ceilings no more than half as high again as the domestic norm still has scope for vertical subdivision.

MEZZANINES

Adding a mezzanine level has structural implications because you are increasing the loads on existing walls. For this reason, it is essential to consult an architect rather than rely solely on a building contractor to carry out the work. An architect will not only be able to specify and design the structure of the new level (perhaps in consultation with a surveyor), but should also be able to suggest various ways in which to make the most of the new space.

Siting is crucial. Don't plan to add a mezzanine level where it will interrupt views or compromise light from existing windows; a blank or end wall is often the best option. You should also consider the sort of space that will be created underneath the new level and what it can be used for. Kitchens, bathrooms, fitted storage and other service areas are often slotted in under mezzanines in order to leave the main living space as free as possible.

A critical factor is the extent of the mezzanine. Think carefully about how you want to use the new area and how those requirements might change in the future before you decide exactly how far the mezzanine should extend into the main space. Very short or narrow

FAR LEFT **ROOFLIGHTS SET IN THE ANGLED PLANE OF THE ROOF ACCENTUATE SPATIAL VOLUME. TOP LIGHTING, WHICH REPLICATES THE NATURAL CONDITIONS EXPERIENCED OUT OF DOORS, IS INHERENTLY EXPANSIVE AND UPLIFTING.**

LEFT **WHERE DOUBLE-HEIGHT SPACE IS SUBDIVIDED VERTICALLY, IT IS OFTEN POSSIBLE TO MAKE A DRAMATIC FEATURE OF A STAIRWAY. THE SWEEPING CURVE OF THIS OPEN METAL STAIRCASE COMPLEMENTS THE CURVE OF THE MEZZANINE AND THE HUGE WINDOW WALL.**

mezzanines or galleries can seriously restrict your options regarding use, but very large ones start to impinge on overall spatial quality.

Another decision concerns whether the level is to be left open, or screened partially or entirely. Open mezzanines provide views through the entire space at the expense of privacy; fully enclosed ones can block valuable natural light. Transparent screens made of glass can be a good solution if you want to keep the overall effect light and open, but require some separation of activities.

Similarly, it is important to consider how the mezzanine will be accessed. Spiral staircases, which take up much less space than conventional stairs, mean that you do not lose much floor area on the lower level. Stairs where the treads are cantilevered out from the wall mean views are minimally interrupted. Perforated metal or metal mesh stairs – or even more theatrically, those of glass – are light and open-looking. You can extend the same material choice to walkways at upper levels. Gridded metal panels or glass panels sandblasted with friction bars set into metal frameworks pursue the same theme of transparency.

PLATFORMS

In situations where the ceilings are high, but not quite double-height, building a platform up from ground level can make space for a high-level bed. Sleeping areas do not require full head height, unless you are the sort of person who feels claustrophobic under a low ceiling, and they do not necessarily have to be particularly extensive – enough room for a mattress with clearance space around the perimeter for access and bed-making is sufficient.

Platforms can be constructed in a variety of ways and from a huge range of materials. The old high-tech standby of scaffolding poles connected with Kee clamps makes a rough-and-ready platform structure; sleeker, more sophisticated platforms can be constructed from timber and fitted with neat kitchen areas, workstations or concealed storage underneath.

BELOW A FLIGHT OF STEPS THAT IS CANTILEVERED FROM THE WALL PROVIDES MINIMAL INTERRUPTION TO AN OPEN SPACE.

RIGHT A SLEEPING PLATFORM SITS UNDER A CURVED VAULT. BY NIGHT, THE SCREENS CAN BE DRAWN UP TO PROVIDE SPECTACULAR VIEWS.

case study

Many lofts come onto the housing market today as shells, where the basic structural conversion has been carried out, but fittings and fixtures are absent and are left for the new owner to select and install. Occupying half of what was formerly a school gymnasium in east London, this loft's initial selling points were its generous height and volume. When the shell went on the market, a spiral staircase linking the ground floor to two new mezzanines had already been added by the original converters of the property. But subsequent design work was required to make the most of the available area and turn the loft into a workable home.

The key advice to making the most of professional skill and input is to choose the right designer in the first place and to provide as clear a brief as possible; in other words, to make sure that both sides are speaking the same language. The new owners of the loft, a professional couple, chose an architect who had been recommended by a builder as one who had considerable flair and experience in exactly these type of conversions. When they went ahead and commissioned the architect to draw up a scheme, they were unambiguous about what they wanted and knew precisely how much they had to spend on the project. The architect, on his part, was familiar with the type

RIGHT AND FAR RIGHT: WITH ITS TWO MEZZANINE LEVELS AND OPEN SPIRAL STAIR, THE LOFT RETAINS A LIGHT AIRY QUALITY. THE PARQUET FLOORING ON THE GROUND LEVEL IS ORIGINAL. THE GLASS SCREEN ON THE MIDDLE LEVEL WAS SPECIALLY COMMISSIONED FROM A SHOPFITTER. MONEY WAS SAVED ON THE KITCHEN FITTINGS BY SPECIFYING STANDARD COMPONENTS.

BELOW: DETAILS MATTER – AND IN BUDGET TERMS, THEY ADD UP. THE CLIENTS ORIGINALLY WANTED GLASS BALUSTRADING FOR THE SPIRAL STAIRCASE, BUT IT WAS VERY EXPENSIVE AND THE ARCHITECT THOUGHT IT WOULD DOMINATE. INSTEAD, THEY SETTLED ON WHITE METAL RAILING, WHICH WAS NOT ONLY CHEAPER BUT ALSO COMPLEMENTED THE STREAMLINED LOOK.

SIDE ELEVATION

SECOND (MEZZANINE) FLOOR

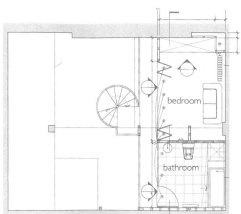

FIRST (MEZZANINE) FLOOR

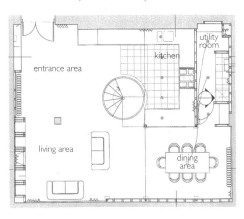

GROUND FLOOR

of look they were after and, equally important, could call on his own trusted and experienced suppliers and builders to keep the work within budget.

The owners had previously lived in a large Victorian house and were keen to retain a feeling of openness in their new loft. Rather than compromise the basic quality of the space with possessions,

the owners specified a streamlined look, with plenty of built-in and concealed storage. The design challenge was to fit in all the accommodation they required – a combined cooking/eating/living area on the ground level, a guest bedroom, bathroom and home office on the middle level, and another bedroom with a shower and steam room on the top – without cluttering up the space.

The starting point for the scheme was to establish exactly how much storage was required. With space at a premium, this could not be quantified on the basis of guesswork alone. The architect asked the couple to inventory and, if necessary, measure their possessions, a process which provided, for example, the useful information that 8 m (26 ft) of clothes rail were required, as well as storage

for 40 pairs of shoes. At the same time, the scheme envisaged extensions to both of the mezzanine floors.

Putting both sides of the equation together resulted in the uncluttered look the owners were after. Built-in alcoves organize books, CDs and other possessions in the living area, while extensive hanging space and shoe storage is concealed behind flush panels on the top level. The architect also proved adept at sticking to the strict budget. Kitchens are potentially a big area of expense, but by working meticulously through the specifications, the architect was able to commission the same kitchen from the same company at a fifth of the original asking price, chiefly by opting for standard rather than top-of-the-range components.

ABOVE LEFT: PIVOTING FROSTED GLASS DOORS ON THE FIRST MEZZANINE SCREEN THE GUEST BEDROOM WITHOUT BLOCKING LIGHT.

ABOVE: THE CLIENTS SPECIFIED SLATE FINISHES IN THE BATHROOM. BY SHOPPING AROUND, THE ARCHITECT WAS ABLE TO PROVIDE THE LOOK THEY WANTED AT THE BEST PRICE. FULLY CLAD IN SLATE, THE SHOWER STALL SERVES AS A MINI WET ROOM.

Natural light

Early enthusiasts of loft living were sold on the quality of natural light that these industrial or commercial premises offered, as much as the sheer floor area. While natural light is particularly valued by artists, it also has significant feel-good factor for the rest of us, animating the interior with subtle shifts and variations throughout the day. The rhythm of these changes connect us with the natural world and make us much more comfortable and at ease with ourselves than the bland, even tones of artificial light.

If natural light promotes a sense of wellbeing, it also enhances our perception of space. Light, airy surroundings always seem bigger and more expansive than areas that are dimly lit or where there is greater reliance on artificial light sources. Part of what makes a loft a loft is good natural light. If you are lucky, your loft will have both larger and more windows, relative to floor area, than a conventional home. In that case, it is simply a question of designing the interior so that light is maximized in the areas where you really need or want it and is not blocked unduly by partitions or other space dividers.

However, lofts with big windows, rooflighting or other similar features command premium prices; so, too, do lofts which are dual aspect. Many of the lofts now on the market are single-aspect, with windows solely along one wall. If the loft is very deep, it can be difficult to bring natural light into those areas furthest from the window wall. The first step is to assess existing conditions of natural

LEFT AND BELOW **LIGHT-REFLECTIVE SURFACES AND FILMY TRANSLUCENT** **WINDOW SCREENS OR DRAPERY MAKE THE MOST OF NATURAL LIGHT.**

light. Where does light come in and how does it change throughout the day? Which direction do principal windows face? What areas receive little or no natural light, no matter what time of day?

Orientation is important. South-facing aspects are warmer, sunnier and more variable than north-facing aspects, where the light is 'whiter' and more even (which is why artists prefer it). East-facing aspects will have sun in the morning; west-facing aspects sun in the afternoon. Plot the path of light through the space and arrange the layout so that daytime activities or main living areas are best lit.

While there may be limited scope for enlarging existing windows or adding new window openings in walls, if your loft is on the top storey, putting in skylights or glazing a portion of the roof can dramatically improve the quality of light.

Toplighting is immensely uplifting, spilling light down through a space in a way that replicates the experience of outdoor light.

If such rooflights can be opened, they will also generate a 'stack effect', whereby air is sucked in from windows at lower level, then warms and rises, escaping out the top. Such patterns of natural ventilation are energizing – they literally 'stir up the air' and help maintain comfortable indoor temperatures when the weather is hot.

Don't block natural light if you can help it. Avoid internal divisions or use partitions of transparent or translucent materials, such as glass, glass block and Perspex. Separate areas, such as bedrooms, can be screened by glass walls that are fitted with blinds (shades) for night-time privacy. If you do need solid partitions, consider puncturing them with internal windows to allow light from adjacent areas to enter. Glossy, reflective surfaces and finishes help accentuate the quality of light. Mirrors multiply the effect of natural light, reflecting into areas of the interior that are not directly lit. Placing a large expanse of mirror at right angles to a window or directly opposite it can almost create the effect of another opening.

You can, however, have too much of a good thing. Big windows bring in the light, but they also put you on show. Unless you have a penthouse loft which is not directly overlooked, you may feel a little exposed. And if you cannot afford to replace existing glazing with high-performance glass, big windows can mean unacceptable heat loss in winter and oppressively high temperatures in summer. For all these reasons, some form of screening is bound to be necessary.

There are a variety of solutions which do not compromise the loft aesthetic. Slatted or Venetian blinds (shades) have a graphic edge, offer a high degree of control over light levels and work well if windows are regularly shaped. Where windows are very high, you can screen the lower portion and still retain good natural light. Roller blinds provide privacy at the lower level yet allow light to stream through above. Similarly, folding shutters or window screens made of Perspex can be fitted against the lower portion of windows. Simple curtains (drapes) made from translucent material or unconventional fabrics work well and provide extra warmth in winter.

LEFT A SLATTED WOODEN WALKWAY
LEADS TO A GLASS DOOR WHICH
OPENS ONTO AN OUTDOOR TERRACE.

RIGHT AN OPEN STAIRCASE AND
INTERNAL SKYLIGHT HELP SPREAD
NATURAL LIGHT FROM LEVEL TO LEVEL.

case study

At least part of the reason why lofts have been so successful is the fact that they do not impose a conventional framework on the way people live. Today, when the boundaries between living and working are not clear cut, adaptable, transformable space keeps step with the fluidity of modern lifestyles. While what most people understand to be a 'true' loft is generally a single open area on one floor, the same flexible approach to spatial planning is beginning to infiltrate other types of residential development.

The conversion of warehouses and factories arranged over several floors into individual single-storey lofts inevitably means that spatial quality will differ enormously between units located on the ground or middle floors and those at the top of the building, where natural light will almost certainly be better. One way round this problem is to convert buildings into several vertical units, rather than divide the space horizontally, so that each loft benefits from ground-floor ease of access and top-floor spatial quality.

This conversion of a former sweet (candy) factory on the southeast coast of Britain features seven four-storey live–work units, marrying the best of the loft and townhouse blueprints. Each unit provides 186 sq m (2,002 sq ft) of space, including 75 sq m

RIGHT: THE UPPER TWO LEVELS OF EACH UNIT HAVE THE SPATIAL QUALITY OF A LOFT, WITH A DOUBLE-HEIGHT LIVING SPACE AND OPEN-PLAN LIVING ARRANGEMENT. THE GLASS BALUSTRADING TO THE MEZZANINE PROVIDES MINIMAL INTERRUPTION OF LIGHT AND VIEWS, AS DOES THE OPEN STAIRCASE.

BELOW: A SERIES OF PORTHOLES INFILLED WITH GLASS PIERCING THE MEZZANINE LEVEL DAPPLE THE SPACE BENEATH WITH LIGHT. THE ROOF TERRACE, ACCESSED FROM THE MEZZANINE, HAS SEA VIEWS.

(807 sq ft) of dedicated workspace on the ground floor. Double doors at the rear of the workspace lead onto a communal Zen garden.

The first floor has two bedrooms and bathrooms, while the upper two storeys provide more of an obvious loft feel, with a double-height living space at the front, a central open-plan kitchen with a dining area to the rear, and a mezzanine level, which provides access through glass doors to a roof terrace.

A cool, natural palette of materials provides a sense of understated luxury: hardwood flooring, limestone worktops, sandblasted glass walls and brushed steel fittings. To complement the flexible layout, the specification allows for remote-controlled sound and lighting systems.

LEFT: EACH LIVE–WORK UNIT COMBINES THE BEST OF BOTH LOFT AND TOWNHOUSE ARCHITECTURAL PATTERNS. THE ENTRANCE AT GROUND LEVEL LEADS TO A WORKSPACE. AT THE REAR IS A COMMUNAL GARDEN. THE FIRST FLOOR COMPRISES TWO BEDROOMS AND TWO BATHROOMS. THE TWO UPPER LEVELS ARE COMBINED TO MAKE A DOUBLE-HEIGHT LIVING SPACE WITH MEZZANINE.

RIGHT: THE FLOOR PLANS OF THE CONVERTED SWEET (CANDY) FACTORY SHOW HOW THE BUILDING HAS BEEN SLICED THROUGH TO ENABLE VERTICAL CONVERSION. THE ORIGINAL BUILDING DATES FROM THE NINETEENTH CENTURY.

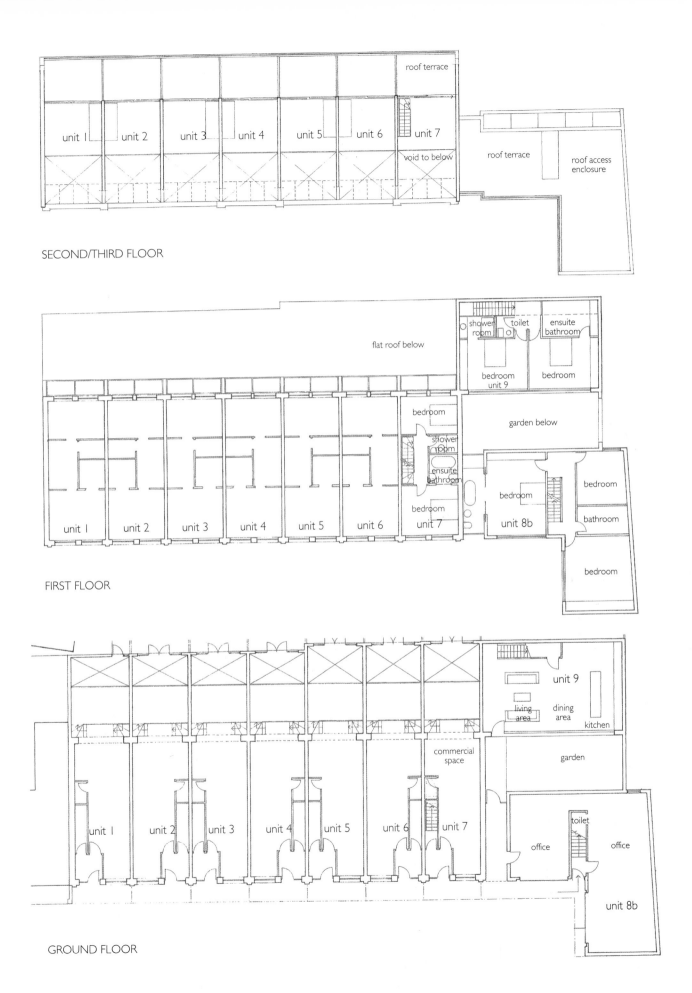

SECOND/THIRD FLOOR

FIRST FLOOR

GROUND FLOOR

case study

With the growing popularity of loft living, a wide variety of redundant buildings have been converted for residential use, ranging from old schools and decommissioned churches to empty factories and warehouses. Few lofts, however, have quite such an unusual past as the Glass House, a stunning reincarnation of what was formerly a secret nuclear bunker.

Standing in an acre of grounds surrounded by woodland, the bunker dates from 1951, a time when escalating tensions between the former Soviet bloc and the West were developing into the Cold War. Built above ground, the concrete walls and ceilings of the bunker are 2.5 m (8 ft) thick to withstand bomb blast: robust, to say the least. As a result, converting the

structure into a light-filled home with a soaring glass roof entailed two solid weeks of diamond-drilling in order to create both the roof opening over the swimming pool and the window reveals.

The Glass House now comprises 647 sq m (6,968 sq ft) of accommodation: a master bedroom with bathroom and dressing room, four further bedrooms (two with adjoining shower rooms), a family-sized Jacuzzi, study, living room, dining room and kitchen. A glass staircase connects the indoor swimming pool on the lower level with the upper reception area and its adjacent landscaped roof garden. State-of-the-art computerized technology, which can be remote-controlled, has been installed throughout. Luxurious materials, ranging from limestone and mosaic to

stainless steel and basalt, have been employed to create sumptuous surfaces and finishes: all in all, a dramatic transformation of what was once a building steeped in foreboding.

RIGHT: A DRAMATIC CURVED GLASS STAIRWAY CONNECTS THE POOL ON THE LOWER LEVEL WITH THE UPPER RECEPTION. THE NEW PITCHED GLAZED ROOF BATHES THE ENTIRE SPACE IN LIGHT; LIGHT REFLECTING FROM THE SURFACE OF THE POOL ADDS A TREMENDOUS SENSE OF VITALITY.

BELOW: FLOOR PLANS OF THE GLASS HOUSE AT LOWER AND UPPER LEVELS. ON THE LOWER LEVEL, ACCOMMODATION IS GROUPED AROUND THE POOL. NOTE THE THICKNESS OF THE WALLS. ON THE UPPER LEVEL, A ROOF GARDEN HAS BEEN DESIGNED TO WRAP ROUND THE CENTRAL VOID AND RECEPTION AREA.

GROUND FLOOR

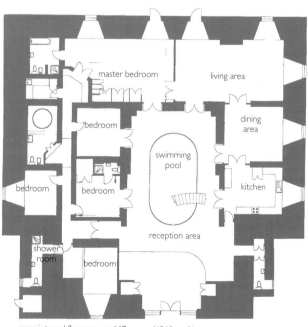

gross internal floor area = 647 sq. ms (6968 sq. ft)

GALLERY FLOOR

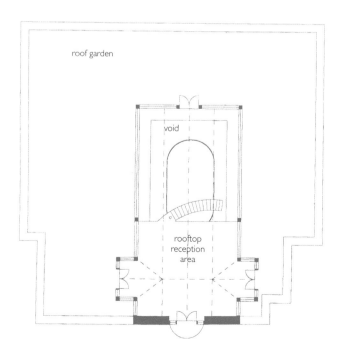

2 decor & design

Decorating a loft brings the quality of materials into focus. This is not altogether surprising – lofts have been largely responsible for the migration of many different materials associated with industrial or commercial contexts into the home in the first place. Then, too, without the reference point of traditional types of detailing, there is increased freedom to play with colour, texture and pattern on a grand scale.

A certain aesthetic has come to be associated with loft living. While early lofts were raw and rough-edged, with evidence of their hard-working origins left defiantly in place, many second-generation lofts display a more reticent approach, as typified by sweeping expanses of wood flooring and white walls. There's nothing wrong with minimalism, if that's what you're after. But if lofts provide scope for alternative ways of configuring space, they also offer possibility for self-expression. When a decorative 'blank canvas' is not conventionally scaled or planned, there is opportunity to give your creative instincts free rein. The most effective lofts are often those with a definitive personal stamp.

Scale and proportion

Big open spaces call for decorative and design strategies that differ from those that might be adopted in more conventional surroundings. When lofts don't work, in terms of decor or design, it is usually because they have been treated as larger versions of the spaces found in ordinary homes. If shaking off a standard approach is difficult, it can be a good idea to start with a neutral background and live with that for a while until you have adjusted to the space and have begun to see its potential. The same is true of furnishing. Don't automatically expect to be able to import furniture that worked in a previous house or apartment; in many cases, such pieces will look marooned in a loft, particularly those that have obvious associations with specific rooms. Similarly, people who approach lofts with a conventional domestic blueprint in mind often seek to reintroduce the type of architectural detailing with which they are familiar, which may be anything from skirting (base) boards to standard-height doors. Such features can rapidly undermine the essential spatial quality that a loft has to offer and result in an uncomfortable hybrid, which is neither one thing nor another.

When decorating and designing a loft, it is of primary importance to shake off the concept of the 'room'. A loft isn't a room that is much bigger, higher or better lit than average; it isn't really a room in a standard sense at all. In conventional terms, a room is a container, enclosed by walls, floor and ceiling. When you're dealing with a loft space, you should think about the ceiling, walls and floor less as boundaries and more as individual planes or surfaces that may be treated in such a way as to unify the space as a whole or, alternatively, picked out to define specific areas of activity.

DESIGN APPROACHES AND THEMES

Keeping the ceiling finish and flooring the same throughout, so that they provide a connecting thread that ties everything together, enhances the sense of space. This is the obvious approach in cases where the planes of ceiling and floor are uninterrupted and in full view. Even where space is subdivided, however, you can still create the same effect. For example, the ceiling will read as a continuous plane if openings in partitions or dividers are full-height (see also pages 26–27). Stopping a partition or wall finish just short of the floor, so the wall seems to hover over it, similarly makes the floor appear uninterrupted; exposing the feet of any built-in storage, such as kitchen cabinets, rather than concealing them behind a plinth, has the same effect.

The secret of successful loft design

is to think big, and think bold.

Changes in flooring, on the other hand, can provide subtle shifts of gear that help locate different areas of activity within an open space. You may also want to use certain types of flooring in specific areas for practical reasons alone – soft, resilient carpet for sleeping areas or hard waterproof tiles in a bathroom, for example. In an open area, combining various floorings often looks best if the materials are the same colour or tone – such as a pale carpet with light hardwood floorboards or stone tiles – and this strategy will also help to maintain an overall feeling of spaciousness. Bolder contrasts of colour generally require more of an obvious boundary, such as that provided by a partition or divider, or by a change in level.

Thinking about walls in terms of planes liberates you from the notion that all four walls must be treated the same. Contrasting colours or surface textures can help to delineate an area within an open space, providing an anchoring backdrop for a dining table or relaxation area, for example. This approach could take the form of an exposed brick wall, or a wall or part of a wall painted a strong colour or clad in wood panelling.

PREVIOUS PAGE **AN EXPOSED BRICK WALL MAY HAVE BECOME A LOFT CLICHÉ BUT IT GIVES DEPTH OF CHARACTER AND PROVIDES AN EFFECTIVE CONTRAST TO SMOOTH PLASTERED SURFACES AND HARDWOOD FLOORING.**

RIGHT **FROSTED GLASS PANELS, INSET WITH A FLAT SCREEN TELEVISION, PROVIDE AN ELEGANT WAY OF SUBDIVIDING SPACE. THE SHIFT FROM LIVING AREA TO KITCHEN IS MARKED BY A SHIFT OF FLOORING FROM WOOD TO MARBLE.**

Above all, the secret of successful loft design is to think big, and bold. Strong colour packs a considerable decorative punch – as does the 'shock of the new' – the frisson of using an unexpected material or finish in an unexpected way. Similarly, thinking big does not mean merely opting for massive pieces of furniture but also looking out for patterns that feature large repeats or overscaled motifs.

In a purely practical way, the sheer amount of surface area you have to decorate may set limits on how much you can do yourself and what you can afford. Spray-painting can make the herculean task of decorating extensive walls less daunting. When choosing materials, you may find more expensive options are ruled out. Instead of downshifting to a cheaper version, it is better to take a sideways step. For example, if you're keen on the cool sophistication of stone but can't afford it, consider polished concrete or a resin floor instead.

Colour

If white walls and loft spaces often seem to go together, it's because white is an unbeatable way of maximizing light and space, and a safe choice. If you really like white, an all-white scheme can have even greater impact, creating a positively ethereal and calming atmosphere.

Fail-safe neutral decorative schemes don't exactly set the pulse racing. Colour may need careful handling but it has a direct line to our emotions. Whereas you might be wary of using bright or intense shades in an ordinary-sized room, and for good reason, the sheer scale of lofts means that there is far less risk that such high-wire strategies will appear dominating or overwhelming, simply because there is so much more breathing space. Single walls, or parts of walls, partitions, doors or other details, can be picked out in bright shades and the vitality of colour enjoyed without running the risk of overkill.

POINTS TO CONSIDER

- **Light tones reflect more light into the interior and enhance the sense of space. Dark tones absorb light and are more enclosing.**

- **Cool colours, such as blue and blue-grey, are 'distancing' and make a space seem bigger. Warm colours, such as reds, yellows and oranges, are 'advancing' and draw in walls.**

- **Clashing colours – red and pink or blue and green – make vibrant combinations.**

- **Before committing yourself to a final choice, take fabric swatches and paint samples home to assess the effect in situ. Be sure to view colours in both natural and artificial lights.**

FAR LEFT A HUGE PHOTO MURAL OF A MOUNTAIN SCENE COMPLETE WITH RUSHING STREAM PROVIDES AN UNUSUAL KITCHEN BACKDROP.

LEFT THE MOVABLE POD, HOUSING A SLEEPING AREA, IS PICKED OUT IN BLUE. ORANGE AND AUBERGINE DELINEATE WALL PLANES.

A VARIETY OF DIFFUSED, CONCEALED
LIGHT SOURCES CREATE GLOWING
BACKGROUND ILLUMINATION, WHILE
AN OVERSIZED FLOOR LAMP PROVIDES
ACCENT LIGHTING IN THE LIVING AREA.

Lighting

Interior lighting is all about lighting spatial volume, a design principle that particularly applies to lofts. Bouncing light off the planes of walls and ceilings – in effect treating these surfaces as giant reflectors – will maximize the sense of space and create a comfortable level of diffused background illumination. Concealed uplighting is a good way of dramatically enhancing double-height areas, literally serving to raise the roof, while spotlights can be trained at walls so that they are washed with light, an effect that

also emphasizes variations in surface texture. In general, such light sources are best hidden or shaded to prevent too great a contrast between bright and dark areas.

Loft-living also offers the opportunity to move away from conventional lighting schemes in favour of more flexible arrangements that delineate specific areas of activity. Try to avoid fixed forms of lighting, such as recessed downlights,

except in areas where layout is itself fixed and permanent, such as kitchens or bathrooms. Bare-wire installations, which allow small, low-energy halogen spots to be positioned anywhere along a length of cabling, are perfect for open, free-form spaces. Another way of keeping lighting flexible is to opt for a series of freestanding table or floor lamps, positioned to create overlapping pools of light and shade which draw the eye through the space. Fit dimmer switches so that you can vary the emphasis; for example, to lower the light levels in a kitchen area when you are eating.

LIGHT SOURCES

The quality of light is key in loft living and this applies just as much to artificial sources as it does to natural light. Most people choose lighting on the basis of the design of the fitting; equally important, however, is the light source itself, in other words the type of bulb (lamp). Different sources render colour in different ways and have a considerable impact on overall atmosphere and mood.

The overwhelming proportion of ordinary household lighting is still provided by the familiar incandescent tungsten bulb, which is cheap and readily available in a wide range of formats, from candle types to globes. Tungsten has a distinctly yellowish or warm cast; it's a flattering, cosy and rather intimate light. If your loft is north-facing and natural light levels are generally rather cool, you may welcome the added warmth and mellowness that tungsten light can supply. On the other hand, if you're after a more hard-edged contemporary look, the richness of this light source can work against it. Tungsten bulbs don't last particularly long; if you use them in lighting that is inaccessible, the need to replace them frequently is a drawback.

Halogen lamps emit a much crisper and whiter light than tungsten. First used in commercial or retail contexts, halogen is particularly good at colour rendering: colours are truer to the way they appear under natural light conditions and not appreciably skewed to one part of the spectrum or another. Small, low-voltage halogen spotlights used as accent lighting can add sparkle and vitality to displayed objects or artwork on walls.

The third most common light source used in the home is fluorescent. Fluorescent sources were once unattractive utility choices; tubes tended to flicker and the light had a distinctly bilious greenish cast overall. Modern fluorescents have greatly improved in their colour rendering, although they still look a little dingy in comparison with tungsten or halogen. Compact fluorescents last virtually forever, can be used in standard lamps and fittings and use much less energy to provide the same level of light.

UTILITY LIGHTING

When industrial buildings were first colonized, loft-living ushered in its own aesthetic: high-tech. As a mainstream decorative style, high-tech may have been short-lived, but lofts still seem to call for a more basic, utilitarian approach when it comes to fittings and fixtures. Large-scale photographic spotlights make good standing lamps; clip-on spots or 'loft lights' deliver bright task lighting wherever required. For a sleeker, less obtrusive look, information lights recessed at the base of the wall or along the edge of the floor create evocatively lit pathways from area to area.

LEFT CONCEALED TUBE FITTINGS, HIDDEN ABOVE AND BELOW A FIXED WALL PANEL, PROVIDE SOFT, ATMOSPHERIC LIGHT FOR THIS BEDROOM.

RIGHT ANGLED TASK LIGHTS, SUCH AS THE CLASSIC ANGLEPOISE, MAKE FLEXIBLE LIGHTS FOR READING OR ANY OTHER ACTIVITY THAT INVOLVES CLOSE WORK AND CONCENTRATION.

DECORATIVE LIGHTING

The scale and proportion of loft spaces and their free, flexible arrangement make them particularly suited to theatrical lighting effects. In recent years, there has been an explosion of interest from designers and consumers alike in decorative light – fittings and fixtures that contribute little to the overall level of illumination but extend basic everyday lighting into an almost sculptural realm. Light wands, nets of fairy lights and unusual light sources, such as neon and ultraviolet, can look faintly ridiculous in a conventional domestic setting but they are perfect for creating a sense of drama in the wide, open spaces of a loft.

State-of-the-art technology also allows you to programme some forms of lighting to change colour and intensity in a given sequence, transforming the interior into a stage set. Such dynamic light shows offer the opportunity to ring the changes as far as atmosphere and mood are concerned, without forcing you to commit yourself to a permanent decorative scheme.

ABOVE FAIRY LIGHTS FESTOON A DECORATIVE METAL STAIRWAY.

RIGHT A LIGHT INSTALLATION DOUBLES AS AN ARTWORK.

FAR RIGHT CONCEALING LIGHT SOURCES BELOW AND ABOVE BUILT-IN WALL PANELS MAKE THEM APPEAR TO HOVER OVER THE FLOOR AND LOOK LESS SOLID.

POINTS TO CONSIDER

· Most areas require a combination of diffused background lighting and directional, focused task lighting. Before you buy a light fitting or lamp, switch it on to see what it does. Don't buy a light on appearance alone.

· Avoid central pendants wherever possible. Enhance the sense of space by bouncing light off walls and ceilings with uplights and spotlights.

· If you do want a central light, opt for branched fittings such as chandeliers or contemporary pendants that have many individual points of light.

· Most homes have too few lights but are overbright. If you increase the number of light sources, but keep individual light levels low, overall illumination will remain the same.

· Create overlapping pools of light and shade to draw the eye through a space.

· Keep lighting flexible. Make sure you have enough power points (outlets) and fit dimmer switches in multipurpose areas. Restrict fixed lighting to permanent layouts, such as kitchens or bathrooms.

· If natural light levels are low, particularly in a work area, daylight-simulation bulbs can help brighten the space.

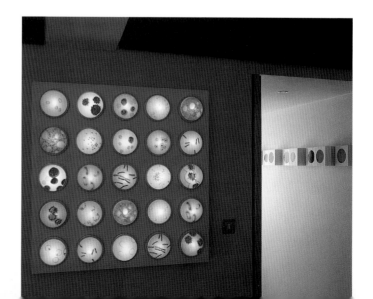

case study

Situated in Hoxton, on the eastern fringes of the City of London, in an area that is renowned for its cutting-edge art galleries and trendy bars and restaurants, this top-floor loft came onto the market as a standard shell, without fittings, fixtures, bathroom or kitchen. To interpret the space, the owner selected an architectural practice whose highly individual work he had seen and admired in an exhibition.

Although the loft is on the top floor and is bathed with light from windows all along the south wall and a roof terrace to the east, it does not offer particularly spacious living space, measuring as it does just 14 m (46 ft) long by 4.5 m (15 ft) wide. The challenge was to convert it into a workable home without losing the light, open quality or the sweeping vistas. By playing with enclosure and

transparency, light and shade, the architects came up with an innovative approach to spatial planning.

Central to the scheme is the slatted bed-box, which serves as the bedroom. This imaginative construction, made from iroko wood, is cantilevered so that it appears to hang in space, stopping short of the ceiling and seeming to hover above the floor. The bed-box is scaled to the size of a large mattress; integral shelves provide space for a television and other bedside items. On one side a hatch folds down to make a desk; on the other the box extends into a wardrobe (closet). There are blinds (shades) which can be lowered to block the light. The appeal of such a design lies not only in the evocative lighting effects that the slatted construction provides, or merely in the look-no-hands character of

RIGHT: THIS NIGHT-TIME VIEW IS OF THE KITCHEN COUNTER IN THE MAIN LIVING AREA, WITH THE INNOVATIVE BED-BOX AT THE FAR END OF THE LOFT SEEN REFLECTED IN THE GLASS DOORS OF THE ROOF TERRACE. ULTRAVIOLET LIGHTS INSTALLED UNDER THE KITCHEN WALL CABINETS GLOW PURPLE. THE EXPANSIVE FLOOR IS OILED IROKO, LIKE THE SLATTED CONSTRUCTIONS.

BELOW FAR RIGHT: THE BED-BOX APPEARS TO HOVER OVER THE FLOOR, ALLOWING THE ENTIRE SPACE TO READ AS A WHOLE.

BELOW RIGHT: A FOLD-DOWN FLAP IN THE BED-BOX SERVES AS A DESK. THE ENTIRE SOUTH WALL IS FILLED WITH WINDOWS.

BELOW: THE FLOOR PLAN OF THE LOFT REVEALS THE LAYOUT AND SHOWS HOW THE BED-BOX MINIMALLY INTERRUPTS THE MAIN FLOOR AREA.

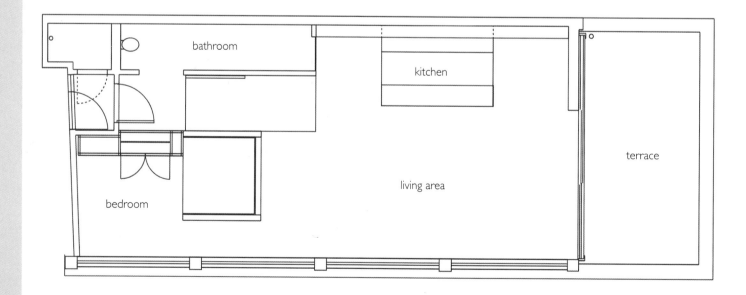

bathroom

kitchen

terrace

living area

bedroom

the structure, but also in the way it evokes childhood memories of dens and hideaways, or 'treehouses' in the architects' estimation.

A similar approach was taken to the design of the kitchen counter, which divides the kitchen area from the rest of the living space and which also houses a pull-out breakfast table. Lights set within the

cabinets. At night, these lights bathe the pure white moulded Corian counter top in an eerie purple glow. A long narrow internal window in the bathroom wall allows moody striped shadows cast by the bed-box through to the bathroom. The bathroom itself is sleekly fitted in white, with white glass panels on the walls and a white poured resin floor.

Shower fittings are up-to-the-minute and include a water-massage mitt and shower-heads that can be angled in any direction.

Iroko wood, used for the bed-box and kitchen counter, is also used on the floor and extends to the adjacent terrace as decking. The terrace is accessed via sliding glass doors framed in galvanized steel.

slatted iroko structure help to dissolve form and reduce what would otherwise have been a rather monumental feature into a shimmering light box.

While the lights within both kitchen and bedroom boxes are tungsten, ultraviolet light is installed under the kitchen wall

ABOVE LEFT: LOOKING TOWARDS THE SOUTH-FACING WALL OF WINDOWS IN THE MAIN LIVING SPACE. THE TWO SLATTED CONSTRUCTIONS OF BED-BOX AND KITCHEN COUNTER DISSOLVE FORM AND ALLOW LIGHT THROUGH.

ABOVE RIGHT: THE GLEAMING WHITE BATHROOM HAS WHITE GLASS PANELS

AND A WHITE POURED RESIN FLOOR. THE LONG HORIZONTAL INTERNAL WINDOW IN THE WALL ALLOWS LIGHT THROUGH.

RIGHT: EXTENSIVE BUILT-IN STORAGE KEEPS THE ENTIRE LOFT CLUTTER-FREE. THE SLATTED CONSTRUCTION STRIPES THE WALL OF THE HALLWAY WITH EVOCATIVE SHADOWS.

Surfaces and finishes

Successful loft design relies less on superficial decorative tricks and effects and more on the choice of materials. Designing with materials provides the opportunity to build in a more robust sense of character; it gives an almost architectural edge to a scheme.

Lofts don't come weighted with baggage in terms of which materials are appropriate and which are not: the field is wide open, which allows you to move away from standard options and explore more innovative and unusual solutions. If your loft is very large, you may also find that upmarket conventional treatments are ruled out on grounds of cost, which is how many of the industrial/commercial material crossovers first came about.

Most people naturally consider a range of different materials when they are making up their minds about flooring. But there are many other applications that are equally relevant: wall cladding, work surfaces and countertops, screens and dividers, and even fixtures and fittings – witness the arrival of bathtubs made of concrete or glass. This breadth of application allows you to set up evocative contrasts of materials, putting sleek clean-lined surfaces such as glass and metal against more rugged finishes like concrete. Many materials these days, including natural materials such as wood and stone, come in a surprisingly wide array of colours and surface patterning, but material quality is often most strongly expressed in textural interplay. This tactile dimension, even if it is only experienced underfoot, adds a subtle sense of depth and rhythm to the interior.

When selecting a material, remember that the choice is not one-dimensional, as it is, for example, when you are choosing a paint colour. Appearance matters, but you should also base your decision on a host of other factors: how the material will perform practically, how it will wear and the maintenance required to keep it in good condition. You will also have to factor in the price of installation and any preparatory work that may be required to underlying surfaces.

WOOD

Versatile, varied, familiar and reassuring, wood is one material we never seem to tire of. Although blonde hardwood flooring looks a little hackneyed these days, there are so many types of wood, in various colours, grains and formats, that fashion need not be an issue.

There are three basic categories of wood and wood products on the market: hardwood, softwood and manufactured woods, such as plywood, wood laminate and medium-density fibreboard (MDF). Hardwoods, which are typically strong, dense and highly attractive, tend to be much more expensive; common examples include oak, maple, beech, ash, cherry, walnut and chestnut, as well as exotic hardwoods, such as wenge, afromosia, mahogany and teak (many of which are endangered, but may be available reclaimed). Softwoods comprise a number of pines and firs that are commonly used in basic construction and joinery, as well as in flooring. Manufactured woods tend to be cheapest. Some, such as high-pressure laminates, perform well; others, like plywood, are not hard-wearing.

FLOORING Not as ungiving as stone, or as soft as carpet, wood strikes a happy medium, combining the clean lines of hard materials with the warmth and tactility of softer options. In a loft space, wood flooring is a good unifier, performing as well in living or sleeping areas as in more hardworking areas such as kitchens. If you want wood over underfloor heating, choose good-quality manufactured wood product, which is more dimensionally stable than solid wood.

If money is not an issue, it is hard to beat solid hardwood floors for beauty, depth of character and the potential to improve with age and use. There's plenty of choice, from narrow woodstrip to wide boards, wood block and parquet. Hardwood must be correctly seasoned before laying and may need to be stored in situ for a period of time to acclimatize. Sealing is essential. New softwood floors are a cheaper option, but they are not as hard-wearing and the decorative range is more limited, unless you bleach, paint or stain them. Protective sealing with several coats of varnish or wax is necessary and the finish will need renewing at intervals.

In a loft space wood flooring is a good unifier, performing just as well in living or sleeping areas as in more hardworking areas such as kitchens.

Many types of wood flooring on the market today are manufactured or composite products, with a veneer layer bonded onto a softwood core. If the veneer is deep, the floor can be refinished at a later date. Laminate wood floors are only nominally wood, and contain plastics and plastic bonding agents to enhance performance. High-pressure laminates are extremely hard-wearing, resist most damage and are easy-maintenance; they also work well over underfloor heating. These advantages, however, must be offset against the loss of authenticity.

If you like the look of wood but can't afford a huge outlay, plywood can be very successful. The thicker grades of ply, faced in attractive woods such as birch, or those which are all-birch, can be tongued-and-grooved and laid like solid wood. Large plywood panels make a seamless, warm and resilient floor; regular sealing prolongs the lifespan to eight to ten years. Bamboo is also a good alternative to wood. Tougher than many hardwoods, bamboo flooring is made from canes that have been pressed, either vertically for a nodular appearance or horizontally for a stripy look. An added bonus is that bamboo, quick-growing and renewable, is environmentally friendly.

WALLS Wood-clad walls are warm and enclosing, offering the snug, clubby look of a den or study. In a loft, it is best to avoid too overt an historical association, which tends to rule out manufactured panelling systems that have been designed to provide a period effect. Instead, opt for seamless wood veneer, plywood or bamboo

LEFT **WOODEN FLOORING IS EASY-GOING AND PROVIDES SCOPE FOR DECORATIVE EFFECTS. HERE, THE ORIGINAL BOARDS HAVE BEEN STAINED DARK BROWN, A TREATMENT THAT ALLOWS THE GRAIN TO SHOW.**

RIGHT, ABOVE AND BELOW **IF YOU CAN'T AFFORD NEW SOLID WOOD FLOORING, PLYWOOD MAKES AN EFFECTIVE, REASONABLY PRACTICAL ALTERNATIVE. CHOOSE THE THICKER GRADES AND SEAL REGULARLY.**

panels for a more sophisticated, svelte appearance. Plain tongue-and-groove panels are another option, but the countrified aesthetic can look out of place in a contemporary space. For a raw and rugged effect, spatial dividers can be faced in strand board, the rough-and-ready product used to board up storefronts or empty buildings.

FIXTURES AND FITTINGS Easy to work with and widely available, wood serves as the principal material for a number of applications, from countertops and work surfaces to shelving and built-in cupboards. Kitchen counters made from the heartwood of hardwoods are strong and durable; for a luxurious effect, seek out the thicker sections. The most streamlined designs are detailed with drainage grooves and overhang inset sinks so there are no awkward joints.

Built-in wooden cabinets vary widely in terms of price and quality, with custom-designed and -built hardwood types at the top of the market and the off-the-peg self-assembly sort (generally veneered softwood) at the mass-market level. A way of upgrading a standard kitchen is to source basic carcasses from a mass-market retailer and have new drawer fronts and doors made in a better-quality wood.

Medium-density fibreboard (MDF) lends itself to all sorts of built-in applications, from door fronts to cupboards and shelving. Stable and uniform, it has a clean, seamless appearance when painted. However, MDF consists of wood particles bonded with plastic resins, including formaldehyde, and there are concerns about its effect on health and the environment, although formaldehyde-free MDF is available. Keep rooms ventilated and wear a mask if you are working with MDF.

If you're after the 'shock of the new', wooden sinks and tubs make a strong statement in bathrooms. Japanese-style hot tubs are generally made from cedarwood, which is both aromatic and antibacterial; sinks may be made of teak or similar hardwoods. Both are very expensive and only available from specialist suppliers.

LEFT **IROKO PANELLING, IN STRIP FORMAT TO MATCH THE FLOORING, HAS A SOPHISTICATED LOOK.**

BELOW LEFT **AMERICAN WALNUT IS USED TO CLAD BOTH A KITCHEN COUNTER AND THE WALL BEHIND THE SINK AND PREPARATION AREA.**

BELOW RIGHT **THE LIGHT TONES OF PALE HARDWOOD CONTRAST WITH WHITE WALLS.**

STONE

Classic, cool and sophisticated, stone brings a calming, rather monumental presence to the interior. Available in a great number of colours, surface patterns, textures and formats, stone is almost always an expensive option and one that generally requires professional installation.

The types of stone commonly used for interior surfaces include marble, granite, slate, limestone and, to a lesser extent, sandstone. Limestone has particular cachet in contemporary interiors because of its subtle neutrality; most limestones are pale and natural in colour and some are marked with the fossilized remains of marine deposits. Strong colour is a feature of granite and marble, both of which take a high polish, while slate, a slightly more affordable option, can be honed or riven and is available in dark, moody shades of blue-green, black and grey.

Stone may seem immutable, but some types are prone to staining, particularly the porous limestone and sandstone. All stones should be sealed before grouting to avoid discoloration.

BELOW **LUMINOUS LIMESTONE SLABS MAKE THE MOST OF A LIGHT-FILLED SLEEPING AREA.**

RIGHT **SLATE IS A PRACTICAL AND GOOD-LOOKING CHOICE FOR KITCHEN FLOORING.**

FLOORING In cooler climates stone flooring undoubtedly works best over underfloor heating, which will take the edge off chilliness. The high thermal mass of stone means that once warmed, a stone floor will retain heat for longer. There are no practical reasons why stone cannot be extended throughout an interior, but it is a hard and resistant surface and can be a little tiring and relentless underfoot. Anything you drop is likely to break and stone will amplify sound.

Stone comes in a variety of formats, from slabs and tiles to small rough setts, which provide grip in wet areas such as bathrooms. The larger the format, the thicker the stone. Stone is very heavy and imposes a greater load on the floor structure than other materials. If your loft has concrete floors, this should pose no problem, but if the subfloor is timber, you will need to seek advice from a surveyor as to whether the structure can take extra weight. Added to the cost of the material itself is the expense of professional laying: installing a stone floor is not a job for the amateur. If you can't afford stone flooring throughout, you might wish to opt for stone in a kitchen area, in an entrance way or as treads on a staircase. Slate is one of the best stones to use for stairs; it has greater lateral strength than other types and so is not prone to cracking.

BELOW **EMPERADOUR MARBLE FLOORING DEFINES A KITCHEN AREA** WITHIN AN EXPANSE OF AMERICAN WALNUT WOODEN FLOORING.

WALLS Stone wall tiles offer an interesting alternative to the more usual ceramic tile finish in areas such as bathrooms, wet rooms and kitchens. Wall tiles can be as thin as 6 mm (¼ in) and tiles up to 1.5 cm (⅝ in) thick can be stuck in place with the appropriate adhesive.

FIXTURES AND FITTINGS Stone countertops and other horizontal surfaces, such as shelves or hearths, are a way of introducing this luxurious material without breaking the bank. For these applications, the stone is available in slabs and may be cut to precise dimensions by the supplier. Most stone counters are available pre-sealed; limestone, however, is particularly prone to staining and granite or marble are better options. The timeless beauty of stone is also perfectly expressed in bathroom fixtures such as basins and tubs, ideal for creating a serene atmosphere as well as sculptural focal points.

CONCRETE

Honest and industrial, almost to the point of brutality, concrete is an uncompromising choice for interior surfaces, but one which has

ABOVE STONE BASINS AND EVEN TUBS ARE INCREASINGLY AVAILABLE.

RIGHT CONCRETE IS USED FOR A SUNKEN BATH AND EXPOSED WALL.

FAR RIGHT A CONCRETE FLOOR HAS NO JOINTS TO JAR THE EYE, SO IT IS VERY CALMING. WHEN COMBINED WITH OTHER MATERIALS, IT HAS A MODERN EDGE.

enjoyed a surprising vogue in recent years. While exposed concrete might seem the polar opposite of a designer finish, it can approach the elegance of stone, particularly when polished.

Many twentieth-century buildings converted into lofts are concrete structures, which means that shells are likely to have at least some integral concrete elements; certainly floors and possibly beams or piers. With minimal treatment, such surfaces can be left to speak for themselves if you like the raw and rugged look. Other applications include countertops, stairs, panels and dividers. Although casting concrete in situ or laying it in the form of tiles is professional work, concrete is a very economic material.

FLOORING Like stone, concrete is a massive material, which means it works well over underfloor heating or insulation. It is also hard, noisy and tiring. Uneven concrete surfaces can be screed with sand and cement. Raw concrete cannot be left unfinished because the surface will continue to 'dust' or break down into fine particles, so some form of sealing is required. Other finishes include special concrete paint and self-levelling resin, which dry to a high gloss. Thin concrete paving tiles can also be laid as a floor over a concrete base.

WALLS AND OTHER USES Concrete is demonstrably a 'poor' or utilitarian material, a familiar and not particularly well-liked component of the urban landscape. Yet in the right application it can

LEFT THIS LOFT HAS PLASTERED WALLS AND LACQUERED MDF CEILING PANELS.

BELOW A PARTITION OF FROSTED GLASS CREATES PRIVACY BUT LETS LIGHT IN.

RIGHT A DRAMATIC UNDERLIT GLASS WALKWAY SPANS THE LENGTH OF THE UPPER STOREY AND HELPS ENHANCE THE SENSE OF LIGHT AND OPENNESS.

have quite considerable textural depth, particularly when studded with indentations or impressions left by casting or formwork. For walls, dividers and other partitions, concrete works best as a rough contrast to sleeker, more sophisticated surfaces, such as plastered walls and polished wood floors. An alternative is to use concrete breeze blocks to build up internal dividers. Individual concrete elements, such as countertops or vanity tops, need to be cast in situ.

PLASTER

Plaster needs no introduction as an interior finish for walls and dividers. In the absence of conventional architectural detailing, though, plaster-work needs to be of particularly high quality: you'll notice if wall planes do not meet at an absolute knife-edge. 'Floating' plaster walls can be achieved by stopping the plasterwork a fraction short of the floor on an inset bead. For softer textural look, plaster can be left undecorated and sealed with a matt varnish or wax to prevent surface dusting.

TERRAZZO

At the opposite end of the price spectrum from concrete, terrazzo is a highly sophisticated finish comprising chippings of marble, stone and glass mixed with concrete or cement. Terrazzo is chiefly used for flooring, where it is poured in situ or laid as tiles; it's very hard-wearing and works well over underfloor heating in cooler regions.

GLASS

Glass means light and openness, qualities particularly prized in contemporary spaces. Increasingly, it also means high performance. Technical advances have recently resulted in an assortment of

types of glass entering the market, including low-E glass which acts as an insulator, glass that turns opaque at the flick of a switch and alarmed glass that incorporates electro-conducting circuits. Added to which, glass can now be manufactured so that it is strong enough to walk on and tough enough not to shatter on impact.

It is small wonder, given these developments, that glass is no longer strictly associated with windows and other openings, but is now used in a variety of ways to add drama and to preserve a sense of transparency in the interior. High-performance glazing is not cheap, however, and unusual specifications, such as glass flooring, will require professional advice and installation.

FLOORING Although, admittedly, somewhat of a challenge for those prone to vertigo, there's nothing more dramatic than glass flooring. It's not a material you would want to use extensively underfoot, but for walkways on upper levels, stairs or in the form of inset panels, glass helps to keep the space light and open while delivering an unbeatable sense of theatricality. For flooring, square metre (yard) panels of thick annealed float glass, comprising a top

layer 2 cm (¾ in) thick laminated to a 1 cm (½ in) thick base, is generally specified; panels are supported in a wooden or metal framework and cushioned around the edges. Stairs can be rather more minimally detailed, but in both cases sandblasted friction spots or stripes are necessary to prevent slipping.

WALLS AND DIVIDERS Glass partitions and walls offer separation of activities without the loss of crucial light. Glass bricks have been around for a considerable time and in recent years have somewhat lost their edge, but they make strong translucent dividers. They are available in degrees of transparency and a selection of colours.

Glass panels or partitions, held within some sort of lightweight framework, can also be used for screening. Select the type of glass according to how much you want to reveal: sandblasted, etched, coloured or translucent glass all provide a degree of obscurity without blocking light. If budget is not an issue, you could opt for the newest type of glass, which turns opaque at the flick of a switch. Safety is also a prime consideration when using glass. Expanses of glass do not 'read' as solid barriers and can lead to accidents. Toughened or laminated glass, which will not shatter on impact, but either break into small harmless pebbles or fracture without splintering into pieces, are the safest options.

Metal means business: a stainless-steel

kitchen implies an almost professional

interest in cooking; metal flooring is instantly

evocative of a factory floor; and metal

stairs and walkways call to mind ship's

companionways or aeronautical design.

FIXTURES AND FITTINGS Transparent and waterproof, glass also lends itself to applications in wet areas such as kitchens and bathrooms, the most attention-seeking of which are glass basins and bathtubs. Glass baths, either moulded as a single unit or constructed of panels fixed with structural sealant, add a completely new dimension to soaking in the tub. There are also contemporary glass sinks on the market; these usually take the form of bowls minimally supported on pedestals or brackets.

More prosaic glass features include tabletops, counters, splashbacks and shelving, all elements with a clean-lined look, which keep the overall effect light and open.

METAL

With its industrial associations and glossy, shiny appearance, metal provides a crisp, modern edge to a scheme. By far the most common metal used in the interior is stainless steel, but zinc, copper and aluminium also have their applications. Of these, stainless steel is the strongest and most expensive; aluminium is lightweight and highly resistant to rust; zinc is highly pliable; and copper has a warm, mellow appearance but is prone to tarnishing. Metal is available in many finishes, from bright polished surfaces to matt burnished ones, and in a variety of enamelled or coated colours. It conducts heat well, so metal surfaces warm quickly and cool rapidly.

Metal means business: a stainless-steel kitchen implies an almost professional interest in cooking; metal flooring is instantly evocative of a factory floor; and metal stairs and walkways call to mind ship's companionways or aeronautical design. Such qualities are perfectly at home in a loft, where they emphasize the origins of the space.

FLOORING Like glass flooring, metal flooring tends to work best in transition areas, such as stairways and walkways on upper levels, particularly in the form of gridded or mesh panels, which provide an element of transparency. Metal floor tiles are also available, in steel or the lighter and cheaper aluminium. To prevent slipping, opt for

relief-textured tiles. Treadplate patterns – the type of surface often seen on factory floors – are most common. Metal flooring is fairly noisy and will heat and cool rapidly.

OTHER USES Sheet metal can be used to clad walls or parts of walls, or as a facing material for counters and built-in cabinets. The most common form of metal cladding is the stainless-steel splashback, now widely available from mass-market outlets. Also available in standard sizes are panels which can be stuck onto door and drawer fronts of ordinary cabinets, providing a cheap and easy way of getting the stainless-steel look. A similar approach can be adopted to clad partitions, closet doors or panels concealing built-in storage.

Used to line walls or ceilings, corrugated metal sheeting makes an overt statement. Steel kitchen and bathroom fixtures – everything from oven ranges and shelving to sinks and lavatories – are both sleek and utilitarian. Zinc makes a characterful alternative to steel. It's easy to bend, so it can be wrapped over counters or tabletops and secured by adhesive or nails. Although it scratches readily, the battered look is part of its appeal.

LEFT STAINLESS-STEEL BATHROOM FITTINGS AND FINISHES HAVE A CRISP, GLOSSY LOOK.

RIGHT SLIGHTLY DISTRESSED STEEL FLOORING PROVIDES AN INDUSTRIAL EDGE.

Decoratively speaking, tiles are a good way of injecting vivid colour into a scheme. In the case of mosaic, strong colour is softened by the tight grid of grouting to produce a luminous, shimmering effect; you can also get mosaic sheet tiling with a random distribution of colours, as well as mirror mosaic for extra glitter and reflection. Single-coloured ceramic tiles are crisp- and contemporary-looking. More striking effects can be achieved by seeking out the new digitally transferred designs, which vary from bold geometric abstract patterns to photographic imagery.

Almost any surface can be tiled, from floors and walls to counters and tabletops. In flooring, tiling particularly suits indoor–outdoor areas where traffic is heavy and places where water-resistance is an asset or a necessity; it can also be combined with underfloor heating to make a warmer surface. With walls, it is important to be generous with tiling – a skimpy splashback or tiled margin around bathroom fixtures looks half-hearted. It is better to extend the tiling to the full height and breadth of the wall, or tile the entire area to make a wet room, for example.

TILES AND MOSAIC

Hard tiles, which include ceramic, terracotta and mosaic, make durable, water-resistant surfaces. The array of formats, colours, textures and patterns offers optimum decorative scope. Because the tile is a repetitive element, a tiled surface is inherently rhythmic and lively; the size of the tile also gives the opportunity to play with contrasting scales. Very small mosaic tiles work surprisingly well in big spaces, providing a tight focus to set against plain expanses. Large tiles, on the other hand, accentuate a feeling of spaciousness.

Tiles are readily available, can be installed by a competent amateur and come in a range of prices, from the cheap and mass-produced to the expensive hand-glazed or hand-shaped varieties. Choose the right one for the job: floor tiles are thicker and more robust than wall tiles and are not as highly glazed, so as to enhance grip.

PLASTIC

Where it is proudly used as a material in its own right, rather than as a shame-faced, cheap stand-in for something more authentic, plastic has an irreverent and retro aesthetic which is perfectly at home in a loft setting. Sheets of translucent Perspex can be framed in wood just as glass can and used as spatial dividers; bright plastic laminates make practical counters and worktops. Cheap plastic furnishings, such as bead curtains, woven strip mats or even astroturf, have tongue-in-cheek appeal. Recycled plastic, striated with splotches of bright colour, is available in sheet and plank form and can be used either as cladding or to fashion worktops and other items of furniture.

RUBBER, LINOLEUM AND VINYL

Available in sheet or tile format, in a host of colours, textures and designs, these materials are almost exclusively used for flooring. They are generally softer, quieter, warmer and more resilient than stone, tile or wood, but the better grades are not necessarily cheaper. Their utilitarian associations work well in loft spaces where they do not need to be restricted to kitchens or bathrooms. For a seamless integrated look, opt for the sheet format rather than tiles.

Rubber, especially studded rubber, is a material with strong high-tech connotations. Hard-wearing and long-lasting, rubber is now available in every conceivable shade: some manufacturers can colour-match any swatch, provided the colour conforms to international colour standards. Marbled or terrazzo effects are also available. Glossy rubber provides the perfect counterbalance to clean contemporary lines, but the textured varieties are more practical since they are less slippery. Rubber can be stained with grease or oil and must be dressed with a proprietary seal.

Linoleum has been upgraded in recent years and has greatly improved practically and decoratively. Although many people erroneously assume linoleum to be a synthetic, it is actually

a wholly natural product and is also antibacterial, antistatic and hypoallergenic. Colours tend to be softer than synthetic counterparts, such as rubber or vinyl, and a mottled appearance is characteristic. Sheet linoleum is heavy and unwieldy to handle; best results are achieved by professional laying.

Although vinyl dominates the cheap end of the flooring market, the best-quality versions can be almost as expensive as a natural material. Many vinyl designs simulate other surfaces – there's even vinyl metal-effect flooring – but it is generally best to avoid the 'lookalikes' and opt for bright colour or graphic pattern instead. Heavy-duty vinyl designed for retail or commercial use – and often impregnated with quartz or granular flakes for slip resistance – has a suitably industrial edge. In a witty departure, vinyl-faced cork tiles are printed with photographic representations of waves, beach stones, leaves, grass and other natural designs.

SALVAGED MATERIALS

A loft, which is essentially a salvaged space, provides the perfect home for reclaimed materials and salvaged fittings and fixtures. Although elements stripped from industrial or commercial contexts often look out of place (and overscaled) in ordinary homes, their robust aesthetic is well suited to spaces that began life as workshops, warehouses or factories.

Most, but not all, salvaged materials are cheaper than new, and they generally have the rugged authenticity that comes from decades of wear and tear, a characterful patina that is almost

LEFT RUBBER IS AVAILABLE IN A HOST OF STRONG CONTEMPORARY COLOURS AND IS EXTREMELY HARD-WEARING PROVIDED IT IS PROPERLY SEALED. THIS POURED RUBBER FLOOR IS SEAMLESS.

ABOVE VINYL IS OFTEN AVAILABLE IN PATTERNS WHICH SIMULATE OTHER MATERIALS, IN THIS CASE LINOLEUM.

RIGHT RECLAIMED CINEMA SEATS PROVIDE AN ORIGINAL TOUCH.

shelving and racking systems organize everyday possessions. There's still a flourishing market in second-hand fittings and fixtures, many of which can be given a new lease of life by refinishing. Old office desks and filing cabinets can be stripped of original paint to reveal polished steel finishes, for example.

Designers such as New York-based architectural practice LOT/EK explore the further reaches of the salvage aesthetic, using heavy-duty scrap to form living pods and enclosures for loft spaces. Old shipping containers, salvaged commercial refrigerators, petrol tanks and cement mixers are transformed into spatial modules for sleeping, relaxing or multimedia entertainment.

SOFT OPTIONS

Many of the materials that have migrated into the domestic repertoire from industrial or commercial contexts are hard and clean-lined. While there's no doubt that such surfaces are more space-enhancing than softer finishes such as carpet and fabric, they do have attendant disadvantages, particularly in terms of noise. If your loft is exclusively finished in hard materials, sound levels can be amplified to an uncomfortable degree, particularly if the space is minimally subdivided. You can, of course, incorporate acoustic insulation into walls, ceilings and floors, but a cheaper strategy is simply to add in a few soft surfaces. While lofts are not spaces anyone would wish to see fully upholstered, draped and carpeted, a judicious use of softer materials provides a welcome visual contrast to all the hard, straight lines as well as an extra degree of comfort and sensuality.

Carpet is an obvious flooring choice, particularly for upper levels or sleeping areas where a little more warmth and resilience is welcome underfoot. Rather than opt for sensible, suburban, neutral shades, make a positive statement with deep textured piles and strong vibrant colour. If you don't want wall-to-wall carpeting, large area rugs perform the same function with the added bonus of flexibility – you can take them up or move them from place to place as need and taste dictate.

Natural fibre flooring – which includes coir, sisal, seagrass and jute – are popular alternatives to carpet. These are quietly neutral

impossible to simulate. Salvage also scores high on ecological grounds: reusing lumber, stone, brick or steel prolongs the useful life of these materials and eases pressure on resources which are difficult to replace or costly in terms of energy to produce.

Architectural salvage yards are good sources of such materials; there are also companies that specialize in reclaimed lumber and stone. Old wooden floorboards are often denailed and remachined in such a way as to retain the original surface. Antique or reclaimed stone, with its appealing depth of character, can, however, be more expensive than new.

Using salvaged fittings and fixtures often involves taking a sideways leap. High-tech was a style that excelled in this type of crossover, borrowing industrial and commercial fittings to use in the home. In this context, test tubes, for example, become bud vases; school lockers and retail store fittings provide clothes storage; industrial

materials, with no obvious associations, and make simple muted backdrops for contemporary living. Jute is the softest and least hard-wearing; sisal can be dyed, which increases the colour and pattern range; coir is very prickly; seagrass is smooth and water-resistant. Natural fibre coverings require stain-inhibition treatments.

Curtains and other forms of drapery are not incompatible with the loft aesthetic, provided you keep the style of treatment simple – no fussy headings and trimmings – and avoid the more conventional furnishing materials (see also pages 28–29). You can hang wide-width material sideways to avoid seams or suspend panels for a banner-like effect.

LEFT SALVAGED OR RETRO MATERIALS AND FURNISHINGS WORK WELL IN A LOFT. THE OLD FASHIONED RADIATOR COMPLEMENTS THE EXISTING METAL DOOR AND BATTERED LEATHER CHAIR.

ABOVE A LARGE STRONGLY COLOURED RUG DEFINES A SEATING AREA WHILE GIVING EXTRA COMFORT UNDERFOOT.

RIGHT A PLATFORM BEDROOM AREA IS SCREENED BY A CURTAIN.

case study

At first sight, this converted factory appears to wear its industrial pedigree on its sleeve. In fact, only the floorboards and staircase are original; the rest of the fixtures, furnishings and even some of the finishes are vintage finds carefully pieced together by the owner, a stylist and shopkeeper who sells retro furniture.

Located in the centre of Melbourne, Australia, the loft used to be a leather-merchant's factory. When the owner acquired it, the building had staircases leading to nowhere and rudimentary services. But as well as the characterful flooring and huge spaces, features such as the large arched window immediately captured her imagination.

The furniture was all salvaged from schools, hospitals and factories: 38 factory pendant lights hang throughout the loft; an industrial workbench takes pride of place in the kitchen. All the fittings, from shower heads and bathtubs down to power points and heaters, come from an old warehouse. The ceilings were refinished in lining boards from an old factory. Modern appliances are concealed behind doors under the staircase.

While it is getting more difficult to find old pieces in good condition, the owner was able to call on restorers to mend, repair and, if necessary, remove top layers of paint to reveal original finishes. Gently battered with the imprint of time, her retro treasures bring out the loft's heritage and rugged character.

LEFT: AN INDUSTRIAL WORKBENCH FROM AN OLD SHOE FACTORY SERVES AS AN ISLAND COUNTER WORK SURFACE IN THE KITCHEN. THE OLD LABORATORY SINK WAS FOUND IN A SALVAGE YARD; TAPS CAME FROM A DOCTOR'S SURGERY. THE VINTAGE GAS OVEN WAS SALVAGED FROM A PUBLIC HOUSE.

RIGHT: AT ONE END OF THE MAIN BEDROOM AN ARCHED DOORWAY FRAMES A DISTANT VIEW OF THE COURTYARD GARDEN. THE ARCHED FRAME WAS ITSELF SALVAGED FROM AN OLD COLONIAL MANSION AND THE SHAPE ECHOES THE LARGE ARCHED WINDOW, ORIGINAL TO THE BUILDING, SITUATED AT THE OPPOSITE END OF THE BEDROOM.

LEFT: THE SITTING AREA ON THE FIRST FLOOR OVERLOOKS A SUNNY COURTYARD GARDEN. A COLLECTION OF WHITE WOODEN VINTAGE CHAIRS SURROUND AN OLD TRESTLE TABLE USED TO DISPLAY PLANTS.

RIGHT: THE DINING AREA, WHICH IMMEDIATELY ADJOINS THE LIVING AREA ON THE GROUND FLOOR, FEATURES A LONG INDUSTRIAL WORKBENCH AS A TABLE AND GARAGE-SALE CHAIRS. THE FAN WAS FOUND IN A FACTORY AND THE LETTERS ON THE WALL WERE ONCE PART OF A BUILDING SIGN. RADIATORS THROUGHOUT THE LOFT ARE ALSO VINTAGE.

BELOW: FIRST- AND GROUND-FLOOR PLANS OF THE LOFT SHOW THE LINEAR LAYOUT.

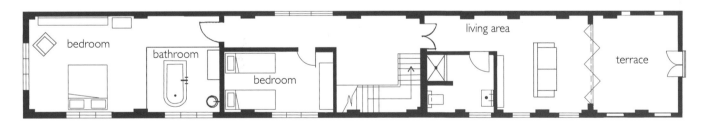

FIRST FLOOR

GROUND FLOOR

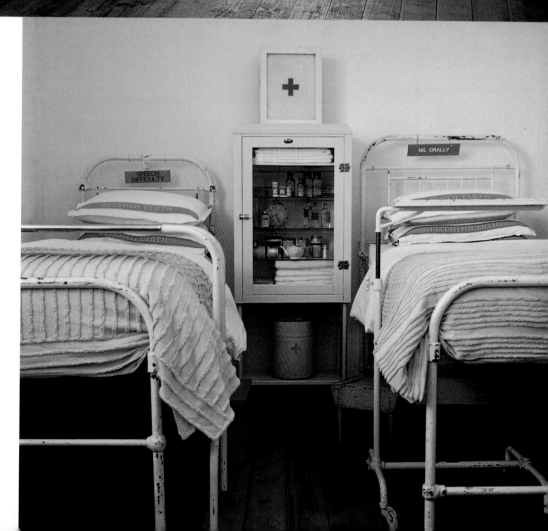

ABOVE: THE ARCHED WINDOW IN THE MAIN BEDROOM WAS ONE OF THE LOFT'S FEW ORIGINAL FEATURES. THE CHEST OF DRAWERS OPPOSITE THE END OF THE BED WAS ONCE USED FOR STORING NAILS.

LEFT: A BATHING AREA ON A RAISED PLATFORM WITHIN THE MAIN BEDROOM FEATURES AN OLD CLAW-FOOT TUB, LEFT RUSTY ON THE OUTSIDE BUT RE-ENAMELLED INSIDE AND FITTED WITH ART DECO TAPS (FAUCETS). A VINTAGE DRESSER (HUTCH) AND A DENTIST'S TROLLEY HOLDS TOILETRIES DECANTED INTO OLD CHEMIST'S JARS.

RIGHT: A PAIR OF HOSPITAL BEDS FURNISH THE GUEST BEDROOM, WITH A MEDICINE CABINET STANDING IN FOR A BEDSIDE TABLE. THE PILLOWCASES ARE MADE FROM TEA TOWELS.

case study

Despite the fact that lofts offer the perfect blank canvas for expressing original design ideas, many are decorated and fitted out in a rather formulaic way. That is emphatically not the case here, where a glamorous live–work space has been fashioned from a basic shell on the second floor of an old printworks.

The spirit behind the transformation is a club designer renowned for his confident and daring use of colour; the shades he has employed here may be more muted than the Pantonesque reds, oranges and

RIGHT: A GLOSSY RESIN FLOOR, EXPANSES OF MIRROR AND OFF-WHITE WALLS CREATE A GLAMOROUS BACKGROUND IN THE MAIN LIVING SPACE. A SEATING AREA IS RAISED ON A PLATFORM. THE COFFEE TABLE IS A HUGE SHEET OF GLASS SET ON A BRUSHED-STEEL DRAWER UNIT. CHOCOLATE-BROWN LEATHER-COVERED SEAT CUSHIONS SURROUND A DINING TABLE. THE SIDE TABLES WITH CIRCULAR CUTOUTS ARE THE OWNER'S OWN DESIGN.

BELOW: A REMOTE-CONTROLLED VOILE CURTAIN SCREENS A SUNKEN LOUNGE AT THE FAR END OF THE LIVING SPACE.

purples that feature in his professional work, but the result is no less individual.

The loft itself comprises 150 sq m (1,614 sq ft) of light, airy space, with a bedroom and adjoining bathroom situated at the far end, a kitchen in the middle and a living area with a sunken lounge occupying the other end. Six months of fitting out followed the loft's purchase, during which time all the basic amenities, from kitchen and bathroom to electrics and heating, were installed, together with new flooring and soft furnishings. But the scheme itself evolved

gradually, the designer preferring to live in the space for a while before committing himself to a particular look.

The living area scheme is white on white: off-white walls and a white resin floor, waxed to a reflective sheen. Because the original warehouse floor was so uneven, the resin kept splitting and had to be redone three times, one of the factors which accounted for the rather protracted fit-out period. The floor itself steps up a level to create a raised platform for the living area and steps down again to make a sunken lounge screened with a

remote-controlled voile curtain. Textural contrasts, from chrome to shag pile, along with the glittery expanses of mirror, prevent the whole effect from appearing too clinical or high-minded.

The kitchen is painted a tranquil shade of lilac, which complements the stainless-steel clad fittings and the exuberant Indian murals bought at a tandoori restaurant clear-out sale. The bedroom scheme was inspired by the mustard colours of the Chinese rug, shades picked up in the hand-dyed velvet-covered panels that make up the headboard

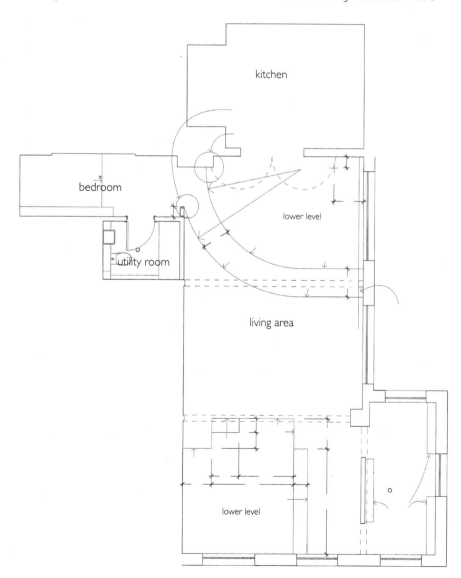

LEFT: THE PLAN OF THE LOFT SHOWS HOW CHANGING FLOOR LEVELS PROVIDES A SHIFT OF EMPHASIS WITHIN THE SPACE.

RIGHT: THE KITCHEN IS PAINTED A CALMING SHADE OF LILAC. INDIAN MURALS, PICKED UP FOR NEXT TO NOTHING AT A RESTAURANT CLEAR-OUT SALE, ADD A TOUCH OF KITSCH. THE BASIC KITCHEN UNITS WERE CLAD IN STAINLESS STEEL TO MATCH THE INDUSTRIAL-STYLE KITCHEN TABLE THAT THE DESIGNER FOUND IN A SKIP.

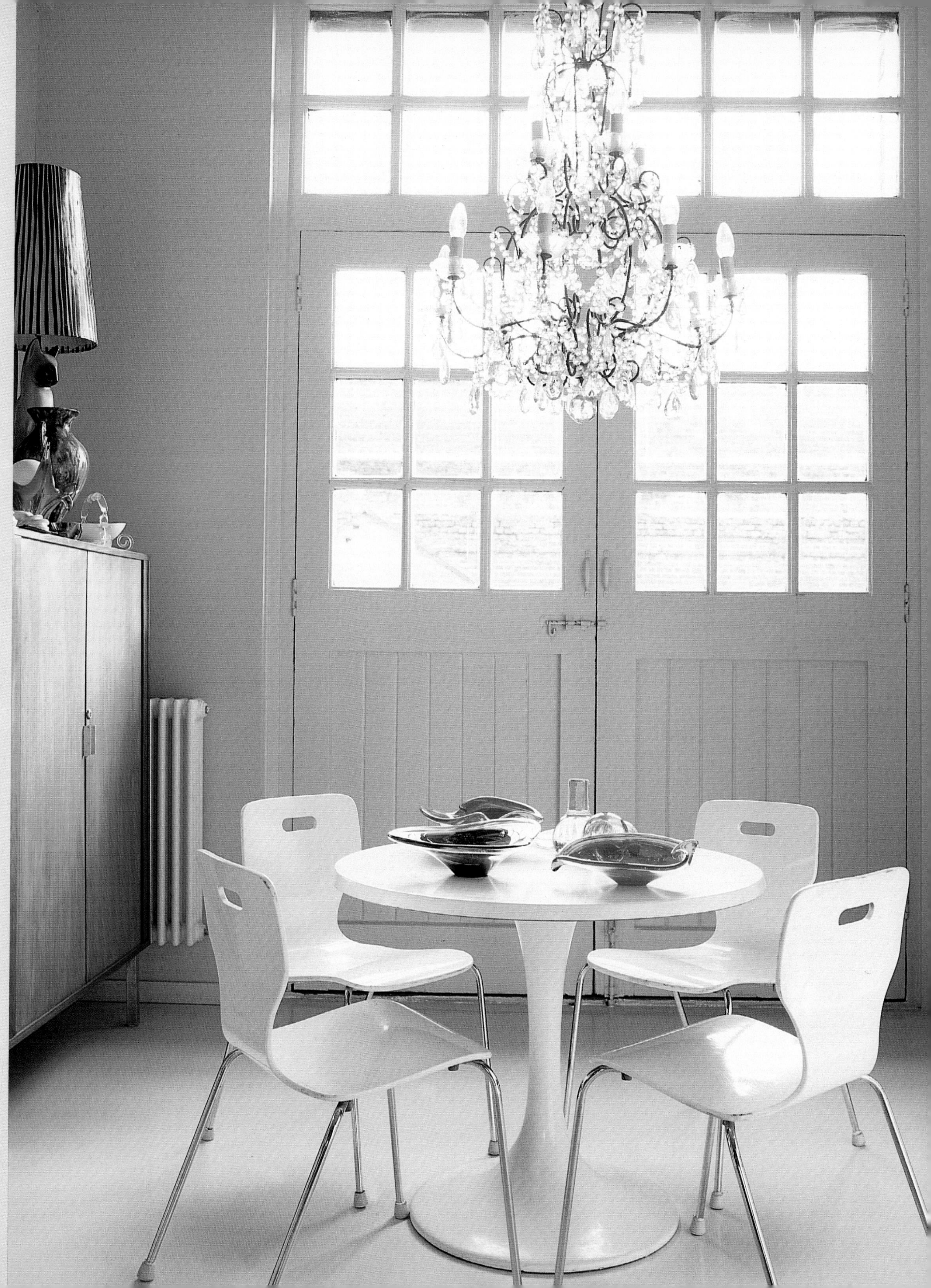

and complemented by the deep purple of the sofa upholstery. The screen, which divides the bedroom from the kitchen and main living area, is finished in silver leaf, making it the perfect backdrop for a Venetian-style mirror that was acquired from a local auction house.

Furnishings are a well-judged blend of retro finds, custom-made fittings and touches of kitsch. Many, such as the Indian lamp bases that serve as bedside lights, were picked up for next to nothing in junk shops or markets. The stainless-steel table in the kitchen was found in a skip. Others, such as the wall light in the lounge and the side tables in the living area, are the owner's original designs.

Since the loft's purchase in 1996, it has had several incarnations and is in constant demand for location shoots. The simplicity of the basic backdrop provides plenty of scope for its designer to explore new ideas in the future.

LEFT: THE EATING AREA FEATURES PLASTIC RETRO CHAIRS, BOUGHT IN A MARKET, AND A GLITTERY CHANDELIER. THE SIDEBOARD IS AN OLD OFFICE FILING CABINET WITH ROLLER DOORS. ORIGINAL DOUBLE DOORS LEAD ONTO A LOADING PLATFORM.

BELOW: THE BEDROOM IS SEPARATED FROM THE KITCHEN BY A PANEL, UPHOLSTERED ON ONE SIDE WITH VELVET-COVERED SQUARES TO FORM A COMFORTABLE HEADBOARD. THE OTHER SIDE IS FINISHED IN SILVER LEAF.

case study

A love affair with the Costa de la Luz, a Spanish region where the decorative influence is heavily North African, inspired one couple to give their loft in central London a distinctly Moorish feel. But rather than express their inspiration in a superficial scattering of cushions, pillows, rugs and other exotic talismans, here, the hot country ambience is more firmly rooted in wonderfully extravagant tilework and vivid colour accents.

When the couple, who have three children, bought the loft, it was an empty shell in a block where other apartments feature the more typical loft palette of glass, steel and exposed brick. Here, however, traditional Moroccan encaustic

tiles provide the unusual decorative signature. The tiles are handmade in Fez and can only be laid two or three at a time; the company which imports them employs Moroccans to carry out this skilled and specialist work.

Although the tiles in the loft are all traditional in design, different patterns are combined to create lively transitions from area to area within the loft. Walls are painted pure white, echoing the whitewashed interiors of Spanish country houses, while the woodwork is picked out in luminous cobalt blue and rich viridian green; the paint was specially mixed to include more pigment so that the final effect was extra-vibrant.

Nearly half of the 160 sq m (1,722 sq ft) space is devoted to a generous, light-filled living area leading onto an open kitchen. In the centre of the loft are grouped three bedrooms, a utility room, bathroom and toilet. Although the loft is mostly arranged on one floor, the children's bedroom is raised up on a platform. Furnishings are kept sparse and simple, in keeping with the Moorish style.

The couple have been holidaying in the Costa de la Luz for 20 years and hope to make a family home there one day. In the meantime, they have managed to distil the essence of their favourite place in their current abode through deceptively simple means.

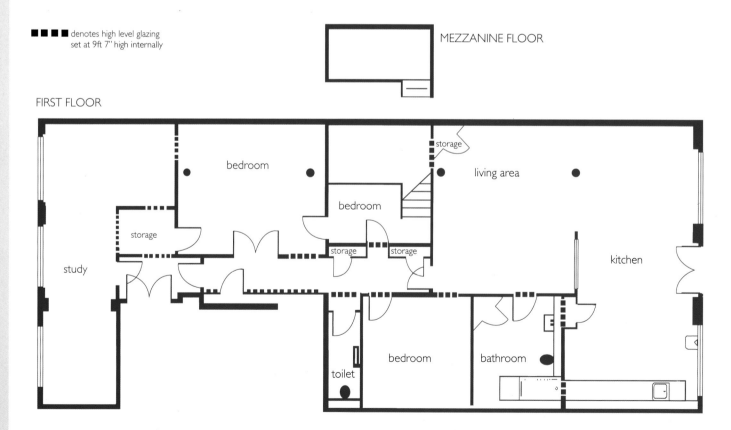

■ ■ ■ ■ denotes high level glazing
set at 9ft 7" high internally

MEZZANINE FLOOR

FIRST FLOOR

THE HALLWAY CONNECTING THE BEDROOMS AND UTILITY AREAS WITH THE MAIN LIVING ROOM FEATURES FLOOR TILES AND TILED SKIRTINGS (BASEBOARD) IN A BOLD CHEQUERED PATTERN. WOODWORK IS PAINTED IN BRIGHT MEDITERRANEAN SHADES. EXTRA PIGMENT WAS ADDED TO THE PAINT MIX TO ENHANCE VIBRANCY.

LEFT: THE THREE BEDROOMS ARE GROUPED IN THE DARKER CENTRAL PORTION OF THE LOFT, AS THIS FLOOR PLAN SHOWS. A STUDY AND THE LIVING AREAS ARE SITUATED AT EITHER END OF THE BUILDING, WHERE THERE IS BETTER NATURAL LIGHT.

LEFT: THE SEPARATE LAVATORY IS CLAD IN BRILLIANT MOROCCAN ENCAUSTIC TILES, HANDMADE IN FEZ. THE TINY WASHBASIN WAS THE SMALLEST THE OWNERS COULD FIND.

RIGHT: MOORISH TILEWORK ON THE FLOOR MAKES AN EXOTIC COMPLEMENT TO EXPOSED BRICK WALLS IN THE MAIN LIVING AREA. THE WALL-HUNG STORAGE CABINETS, HOUSING A MUSIC SYSTEM, BOOKS AND MAGAZINES, ARE ACTUALLY KITCHEN CABINETS.

BELOW: THE MAIN BEDROOM IS SIMPLY FURNISHED WITH A PEG RAIL, FLOOR-LEVEL BED AND WOVEN NORTH AFRICAN COVER. THE INTERNAL WINDOW, SIMILAR TO THOSE IN SPANISH HOUSES, LETS IN LIGHT AND BREEZES.

case study

One way of tackling the issue of how to subdivide space within a loft is to hive off activities that require a little privacy or self-containment into pods or modules. The particular advantage of this approach is that it provides an element of enclosure without compromising the exhilarating scale and proportions of a big space. While this is not a strategy that is going to work in conventionally scaled interiors, the sheer volume and size of a loft guarantees its success.

In this loft apartment, located in New York's West Village, the pod is actually an oil tanker, refashioned by an architectural practice that specializes in exploring the further reaches of creative salvage. Now serving as a bedroom for the loft's owner, the pod was originally an 11-m (35-ft) long tank from an oil truck with a capacity of 32,728 litres (7,200 gallons). The architects bought it secondhand in New Jersey and had it thoroughly steam-cleaned before splitting it into two sections, one of which became the bedroom, while the other was used vertically to enclose a bathroom. Both sections had to be hoisted through the loft's window by a crane.

RIGHT: A METAL GRILLE WALKWAY PROVIDES ACCESS TO THE POD, WHOSE INTERIOR IS PAINTED INTENSE CHROME YELLOW.

BELOW: THE BEDROOM POD IS POSITIONED AT MEZZANINE HEIGHT, BRIDGING THE VAST OPEN SPACE OF THE LOFT AND RESEMBLING AN ENORMOUS OVERSIZED HEATING DUCT. FURNISHINGS ARE KEPT DELIBERATELY HARD-EDGED AND INDUSTRIAL TO COMPLEMENT THIS EXTRAORDINARY STRUCTURE: THE LOCKERS, CABINETS AND TABLES ARE METAL AND THE CHAIRS ARE OF A DESIGN USED IN PRISONS AND OTHER INSTITUTIONS. GLOSSY HIGH-TECH FINISHES ADD SPLASHES OF COLOUR.

The bedroom pod, which crosses the loft like a giant duct or pipeline, has hydraulically powered flaps on either side to provide access to the interior, with fitted mattresses that fill the available space. The pod is reached via a metal ladder and gangway that wraps around the second, vertical pod housing the bathroom. A peephole in the bathroom pod provides a view of the kitchen. The rugged, heavy-duty industrial look of the loft is accentuated by factory finishes. The interior of bedroom pod is spray-painted with bright yellow car paint, while the floor of the main living space is poured epoxy resin in a strong shade of blue.

RIGHT: HYDRAULICALLY OPERATED FLAPS PROVIDE ACCESS TO THE INTERIOR OF THE BEDROOM POD, WHICH RESTS ON STEEL BRACKETS SUPPORTED BY A STEEL BEAM.

BELOW: FLOOR PLANS OF THE LOFT SHOW THE CIRCULAR FORM OF THE BATHROOM MODULE AND THE POSITIONING OF THE BEDROOM POD.

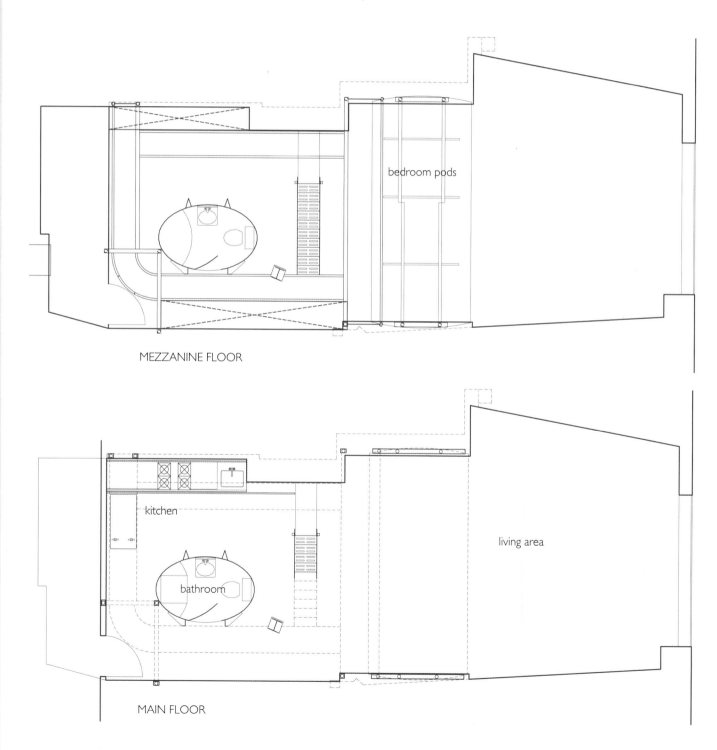

bedroom pods

MEZZANINE FLOOR

kitchen

living area

bathroom

MAIN FLOOR

Focal points and features

All interiors need a focus, and the larger and more open the space, the more important it is to draw everything together into a cohesive whole. A focal point or feature does not literally have to occupy centre stage, but it must be dominant enough to read clearly from all parts of the interior – a picture or rug that looks like a postage stamp from the other side of the room is not going to do the trick, however stunning it might be at close quarters. Remember, too, that volume comes into the equation. Size matters, but so does height. Breaking up a collection of low-slung furniture with a tall piece adds definition; treating a single wall as a designated floor-to-ceiling display area, or even storage area, also breaks up what might otherwise be a featureless expanse.

Focal points in a loft setting are less about creating centrepieces and more about putting down spatial markers, points of orientation that make sense of a wide open space. In a conventional interior, a big sofa can serve as an impressive spatial marker. In a loft, you would need a very large sofa indeed to make that same sort of impact. Here, it can be a good idea to think laterally – instead of a traditionally shaped sofa, consider more extensive sectional seating to describe and delineate a relaxation zone. Rather than dotting pictures and paintings around the place where their effect will be diluted, group them in a single collection on one wall, where they will have greater presence. On the lighting front, try substituting a cascade of fairy lights or an outsize factory fitting for a standard-sized chandelier or decorative pendant.

The fireplace has long been a traditional point of focus in the home and the word 'focus' in Latin itself means 'hearth'. Given their commercial or industrial pasts, few lofts incorporate fireplaces as part of the original detailing but that does not necessarily mean you have to forego the physical and psychological comfort of a real fire. Contemporary stoves and fires, with their bold sculptural forms, make strong statements in their own right, as well as deliver additional heat. Many incorporate integral flues in their design, which means they can be placed in the centre of a room.

Scale is an important criterion, but it is not the only one. If lofts liberate you from normal space standards and arrangement, they also free you from the dead hand of 'good taste'. A loft provides an ideal setting for any whimsy – whether it is a large tropical fishtank, a retro neon sign or a kitsch cocktail cabinet. You can turn an entire wall into a work of art by blowing up a favourite photograph and sticking it to the wall to create a photomural. With no conventional precedents in terms of decor and design, the perfect opportunity exists to indulge in personal expression.

LEFT THIS BUILT-IN ARRANGEMENT COMBINES THE TRADITIONAL FOCUS OF THE HEARTH WITH THE INEVITABLE MODERN FOCUS OF THE TELEVISION. A STACKING MUSIC SYSTEM IS TO THE RIGHT.

RIGHT IN MORE OF A CASUAL, FREE-FORM USE OF SPACE, CLOTHES AND COSTUMES ARE HUNG ON CLOTHES RAILS LIKE DECORATIVE OBJECTS, SCREENING THE VIEW OF THE BED.

case study

Proof, if it were needed, that loft living has come of age, this New York loft is actually a reworking of a previous loft conversion, carried out 20 years ago when the movement was taking off. Situated on the top floor of the Eagle Warehouse in Brooklyn Heights, the space is dominated by a magnificent glass clockface providing sweeping views of Brooklyn Bridge and the Manhattan skyline.

The building in which the loft is located began life as the headquarters of the Brooklyn Eagle, a newspaper which was edited in the mid-nineteenth century by the celebrated American poet Walt

Whitman. At the end of the nineteenth century, the building was extensively renovated and converted into a warehouse providing storage for middle-class families moving into Brooklyn to escape Manhattan's rapidly escalating land values. Brooklyn

RIGHT: THE MAIN SPACE IS DOMINATED BY THE GLASS CLOCKFACE. ADDITIONAL NATURAL LIGHT IS PROVIDED BY TWO ENORMOUS SKYLIGHTS, ONE IN THIS AREA AND ONE IN THE BEDROOM. FURNITURE IS A MIXTURE OF ENGLISH, FRENCH AND AMERICAN ANTIQUES.

BELOW: THE BUILDING IS LOCATED AT THE BASE OF BROOKLYN BRIDGE.

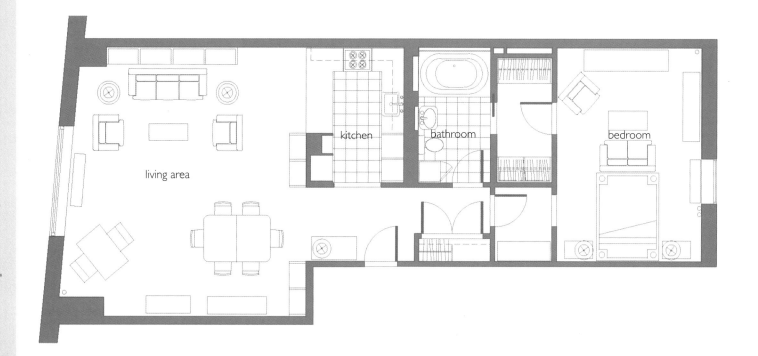

living area

kitchen

bathroom

bedroom

Bridge was being constructed at the same time and when the architect of the renovation realized that the deck of the bridge would be more or less level with the top floor of the building, he added the clock, whose face advertises the company's name.

Rundown and abandoned in the 1980s, Eagle Warehouse was a prime candidate for developers cashing in on the loft boom. A condition of converting the property was that it was 'landmarked' or given heritage status. However, when the present owner, an architect and interior designer, moved in, very little of the original character had been maintained. The loft was subdivided into individual rooms, the ceiling had been lowered by 1.5 m (5 ft), partially obscuring the clockface, and interior surfaces were concealed behind plasterboard.

The owner's response was to re-imagine the space as if the original architect had designed it for himself. He stripped away the partitions and false ceiling, took the walls back to the brick and transformed what had been a two-bedroom apartment into a one-bedroom loft. Over half the floor area is now an open space, where different functions are defined by lighting, cabinets and counters, and furniture placement. With the original scale and proportions restored, the sprinkler pipes, valves, and clockface, along with its motor and steel strapping, fully exposed, the result was a return to a true loft space.

OPPOSITE, TOP: THE REDESIGNED LOFT HAS AN OPEN LIVING/EATING/SLEEPING AREA, A CENTRAL BATHROOM AND A BEDROOM TO THE REAR. A LOBBY ACTS AS A TRANSITION BETWEEN THE PRIVATE AND PUBLIC AREAS.

OPPOSITE, BELOW: 'EAGLE WAREHOUSE & STORAGE COMPANY OF BROOKLYN': THE VIEW OF THE LOFT, WITH THE CENTRAL CLOCKFACE, FROM BROOKLYN BRIDGE.

ABOVE LEFT: FURNISHINGS REVEAL A FASCINATION WITH TURKOMAN AND CENTRAL ASIAN CARPETS AND TEXTILES, A FASCINATION FUELLED BY REGULAR BUYING TRIPS TO TURKEY.

ABOVE RIGHT: THE BEDROOM HAS AN EASTERN FEEL, WITH PILES OF CUSHIONS, PILLOWS AND TEXTILES, AND A MOROCCAN-STYLE LANTERN.

3 zones

Loft-living requires a new mind-set, the ability to 'think out of the box'. To get the most from the space you need to analyse the patterns of different activities so they flow logically from one area, or zone, into the next. At the same time, ingenious 'transformable' fixtures and furnishings allow space to be adapted. Increasingly what we require our homes to provide is flexibility. Flexible space allows you to spend nights in front of the television – or throw a party for friends. Flexible space lets you work at home or have guests to stay without turning the whole household upside down. Flexible space doesn't dictate how and when you use zones within it, but supplies an elastic framework that supports the way you want to live.

Good, workable storage systems are essential to free space and promote an uncluttered look. You don't have to be minimalist or reduce your possessions to bare necessities but it is important not to treat a loft as a warehouse for belongings. Think about what you really want and need, and reject what is surplus to requirements. And, finally, although lofts originated as an urban phenomenon, many afford at least some scope for outdoor living, via a roof garden or balcony. Alternatively, one way of enjoying nature is simply to bring it indoors.

Storage

Deciding how and where you keep your belongings should never be an afterthought. Storage is not just about tidying possessions away; it is integral to the way that a space works. In a loft, good storage is often the primary means of maintaining a feeling of spaciousness. But it's not enough to create a clutter-free look, storage must also be fundamentally workable. While it is possible to create seamless cupboards to hide all your belongings, that may not necessarily be the best way to support different activities. A system that is difficult to use won't be used, and you'll leave things lying in view anyway, defeating the point of the exercise. The workability of storage is particularly critical for those things you need on a daily basis.

Storage is not just about tidying possessions away; it is integral to the way that a space works.

In older houses, built at a time when people had fewer possessions, storage space is often very limited. A loft, however, allows you to consider storage right from the outset. You should also take the time to evaluate your belongings and dispose of those that you don't really need. If you can never have too much storage space, it is also true that you can always do with fewer things: somewhere there is the perfect meeting point between the two.

Moving into a loft provides the ideal opportunity to take a long hard look at what you've been hanging onto and determine whether it really does merit the house room. Possessions come with emotional baggage and can be hard to let go. The type of articles people tend to have the most difficulty parting with are those that inspire guilt, a category that embraces unwanted gifts, unread books, clothing that doesn't fit or styles that don't work, as well as items that are broken and awaiting repair or simply unfortunate impulse buys. Clearing the decks of such possessions can be a spiritual 'spring clean' and make you appreciate the belongings you keep all the more.

The next step is to analyse your belongings in terms of how often you use them and how accessible they need to be. Whereas it is no trouble to retrieve an item from a remote location if it is used only seasonally or once a year, it is infinitely frustrating to be unable to access items on daily call freely and easily. Things you use regularly need to be kept as close as possible to the area where you use them. Candidates for deep storage include: Christmas decorations; tax returns and any other documents you must keep for statutory purposes; out-of-season sports equipment and clothing; catering-sized kitchen equipment or dishes if you don't entertain frequently.

PREVIOUS PAGE A SLIDING PARTITION PICKED OUT IN BRIGHT RED PROVIDES FLEXIBLE DIVISION, SIGNALLING THE SHIFT FROM ONE AREA OF THE LOFT TO THE OTHER. BUILT-IN SHELVES PROVIDE EXTENSIVE STORAGE FOR CDS.

LEFT AND RIGHT THESE FIXED STORAGE UNITS MADE OF PURPLE HEARTWOOD HAVE A SCULPTURAL PRESENCE. THE UNITS, WHICH HAVE INVISIBLE DOORS, PROVIDE INCONSPICUOUS STORAGE AND CREATE A CORRIDOR BETWEEN A DINING AREA AND A CLOAKROOM.

BUILT-IN STORAGE

Open-plan multipurpose spaces offer maximum scope for clever, integrated storage solutions. When you are not constrained by a layout based around separate rooms, storage can be conceived almost in an architectural fashion as part of the working fabric of the space as a whole. Such built-in features can be the means by which different areas of activity or zones are defined and they will also mean that you need less in the way of freestanding furniture, which helps to keep floor space clear. The cardinal rule when it comes to integrating built-in storage within a large open space is to be wholehearted about it and avoid dotting it about from

LEFT CORRIDORS PROVIDE IDEAL SPACE FOR CONCEALED STORAGE. HERE, AN ENTIRE WALL OF BUILT-IN CUPBOARDS IS HIDDEN BEHIND WOODEN PANELS, WITH OPEN SHELVING IN ADJACENT AREAS.

RIGHT CUSTOM-BUILT METAL-CLAD STORAGE KEEPS CLUTTER FROM VIEW.

BELOW FLUSH PANELS CONCEAL STORAGE AREAS FOR THE ULTIMATE SEAMLESS LOOK.

place to place in an ad hoc fashion. Running low-level cupboards the entire length of a wall, or shelving a wall from top to bottom, makes the entire effect look well-considered and streamlined.

In traditional homes, existing structural features often suggest a location for built-in storage; alcoves either side of a fireplace, for example, are natural sites for shelving or closed cupboards. But in a regular-shaped shell devoid of such architectural pointers you start with a blank canvas and so you may need to think laterally. It may be more the case of choosing to devote an entire wall to storage or building dividers or partitions that double up as storage areas, preferably on both sides. Mini storage 'rooms' such as walk-in closets, dressing rooms or pantries can be highly effective in open-plan spaces, providing a tailor-made means of organizing possessions with optimum spatial economy.

Concealed storage is a good idea in lofts that are not particularly generous in terms of floor area. At their most seamless, cupboards and shelving can be hidden behind flush panels that close on press catches, with no visible hinges or handles to indicate their presence. When all the doors are closed they look like a flat wall. But such storage needs to be well-planned and sited to ensure its workability and you will need to be a fairly organized person or you will be constantly opening and closing doors trying to locate the bed linen or remembering where you put the computer games.

OPEN STORAGE

While standard and familiar items of storage furniture – such as closets, chests of drawers and other traditional pieces – can look clumsy and out of place, borrowings from commercial or retail spheres look much more at home in a loft. Industrial or catering-style open metal shelving units can provide a robust way of organizing everything from books and music equipment to kitchen paraphernalia and utensils; glass-fronted display cabinets can be used to store clothing or linens. For a rough-and-ready aesthetic, old metal lockers or filing cabinets are practical catch-alls.

A good strategy for stowing away clutter is to use a series of containers: a neat array of uniformly shaped boxes can help organize disparate items in a logical way. Uniformity is the key: choose one style of container and use it throughout the space. Many retailers market ranges of containers in different materials, from stout cardboard to plastic, metal to luxurious leather, so achieving a coordinated look is not difficult.

Open storage – where storage meets display – animates any interior and lofts are no exception. A wall of neatly shelved and brightly jacketed books has a rhythmic, textural quality. Similarly, hanging kitchen utensils from a metal rail or outdoor gear from a row of pegs adds an essential touch of life that prevents the overall effect from looking too uptight and clinical.

LEFT A STORAGE UNIT ORGANIZES A COLLECTION OF CDS. THE MOST EFFECTIVE STORAGE IS THAT WHICH IS TAILORED TO THE SIZE AND DIMENSIONS OF WHAT YOU INTEND TO PUT INTO IT.

RIGHT UNIFORM CONTAINERS, SUCH AS THESE WOODEN BOXES, HAVE A CLEAN-CUT ANONYMOUS LOOK WHICH PREVENTS UNFITTED STORAGE SOLUTIONS FROM LOOKING TOO OBTRUSIVE.

Creating transformable space

An open multipurpose space such as a loft is inherently transformable. When most day-to-day activities occur within the same area, the shift of emphasis occurs naturally through the course of the day: when you sit down to eat, it's a dining area; when you lounge in front of the television, it's a chill-out zone; when you tackle paperwork, it's a home office.

This is all well and good if you're on your own or if there are just two of you sharing the space. Factor more people into the equation, however, and the potential for conflict increases. When friends drop by for a chat, your partner is trying to prepare an important report and the kids are playing Nintendo all within the same four walls it's a recipe for muddle and mayhem. Similarly, when guests come to stay – and with the plurality of modern households those guests might be anyone from your best friend to the mother-in-law to stepchildren – the spatial arrangements that worked so seamlessly for one or two may be severely stretched.

Space is not infinitely transformable, but there are a number of ways in which you can increase flexibility. One strategy is to literally build it in, in the form of movable partitions, screens and fitted elements. The second is to furnish the space with pieces that are transformable or multipurpose in themselves.

BUILT-IN FLEXIBILITY

Designers of flexible, transformable places treat the basic shell of the loft rather like an articulated box – or an exercise in origami. Walls or panels can be swung out to subdivide the space in a number of different ways and then folded back into place when you want the space to be open again. The core of many such designs is the servicing, with kitchen and bathroom areas providing the fixed point of the layout and built-in storage and other fitted elements lining the walls. A similar approach can be seen in the design of one New York apartment, where a double workstation is housed in a freestanding cabinet; full-height panels can be swung open when the space is in 'office' mode and shut again at night so that work is out of sight and does not impinge on the living space.

The success of such transformable designs relies on precision detailing and construction, which means that you will not only need an architect or designer to come up with the scheme, but one who also has a good track record in making transformable spaces really work. If you need to be able to switch a space from office to home and back again every day, or to reconfigure it to accommodate one, two or more separate areas, then wall panels, screens or other built-in elements must be robust, easy to operate and dovetailed. Less complex arrangements rely on sliding screens – run along ceiling or floor tracks, for example – or similar partitions to enclose different zones as required and provide the necessary degree of privacy (for further ideas on dividing space, see pages 24–29).

Flexible walls and dividers can be complemented with built-in elements, such as foldaway (Murphy) beds and flap-down tables or desks. Foldaway beds used to be notoriously unreliable, but new designs have secure anchorages and counterbalanced spring mechanisms to ensure there are no sudden surprises. Fold- or flap-down panels are space-saving and versatile; depending on size, positioning and robustness, they can serve as additional kitchen work surfaces, dining tables, seating, bedside tables or desks – anything that requires a stable flat surface. The more fitted elements of this nature you can build into the space, the less furniture you will require, which helps to keep everything light and open.

FLEXIBLE FURNITURE

What you put into a loft in the way of furnishings can also go a long way towards increasing flexibility of use. In general, lofts call for a different approach to furnishing from a standard house or apartment. Aside from issues to do with scale, there is also the need to avoid furniture styles that are essentially room-specific. A table that too obviously cries out to be the centrepiece of a formal

RIGHT THE KEY TO TRANSFORMABLE SPACE IS PRECISION DETAILING AND CONSTRUCTION TO MAKE SURE THAT FEATURES, SUCH AS THIS MOVABLE BEDROOM PARTITION, REALLY WORK, IN OTHER WORDS, THAT THEY FIT NEATLY INTO PLACE AND ARE EASY TO OPERATE.

An open multipurpose space, such

as a loft, is inherently transformable.

dining room will look ridiculous in a loft. However, a table whose design is distilled to the most basic and functional elements – a flat surface resting on supports – can serve as an additional kitchen work surface, eating area and desk, and look the part whatever the role.

What you put into a loft in the way of furnishings can also go a long way towards increasing flexibility of use.

Modular furniture, such as storage cubes or sectional seating, is perfect for loft spaces because it allows you to expand, adapt and reconfigure according to need. Individual modules are anonymous enough to go anywhere and such designs often provide more true versatility than multipurpose furniture, such as sofabeds. Modernist designers have long focused on basic adaptable forms – it's hard to beat Alvar Aalto's classic stool, for example, which can be used as an occasional table or seating, and stacked when not in use. Stacking or folding chairs that can be used indoors or out, as dining chairs or additional seating, in living areas or bedrooms, are another good example of truly multipurpose furniture.

More recently, the whole notion of transformable furniture has caught the imagination of a new generation of furniture designers and there are some ingenious products on the market: tables that can be transformed into chests, and so on. Many of these are more in the nature of playful and witty exercises than practical solutions but this is a definite trend that looks set to continue. On a more basic level, flexible furniture can be as simple as stacking floor cushions that unfold to create a mattress, or beds with drawers in the base for additional storage. The simplest designs often function the best.

LEFT AND ABOVE LEFT **FEATURES SUCH AS FOLD-DOWN BEDS GIVE YOU TWO SPACES FOR THE PRICE OF ONE.**

ABOVE RIGHT **A BREAKFAST BAR PULLS OUT OF A KITCHEN COUNTER.**

RIGHT **ALVAR AALTO'S CLASSIC STACKING STOOL CAN DOUBLE UP AS A BEDSIDE OR OCCASIONAL TABLE.**

Live–work

Using a loft as a workspace completes the circle in many ways. After all, true lofts originated as workspaces and the hard-edged aesthetic is what many people have found attractive about them in the first place. Lofts come with plenty of inherent advantages for those wishing to work from home. Aside from their nondomestic qualities, which make work areas less of an obvious intrusion, there is also the relatively unstructured nature of the space, which means fewer restrictions when it comes to planning and equipping a work zone.

Lofts come with plenty of inherent advantages for those wishing to work from home.

Preliminary planning and assessment are critical. When you're working and living in the same space, it is important to ensure that one part of your life does not impinge on the other. If the work side dominates, you may never really get the chance to relax and unwind, or to bring the fresh perspective to your work that a little psychological distance provides. If the home side gets the upper hand, your productivity – and career prospects – may be seriously affected. To get the balance right, you need to think carefully about the type of work you do, what it requires in terms of servicing and equipment, and the conditions you require to work at your best. 'Working from home' is a broad continuum that stretches from the occasional break from office routine to catch up on work that requires more dedicated concentration to the fully fledged home business. Bear in mind that whatever your arrangements are at the moment, circumstances and preferences can change in the future, so be sure to build in a little flexibility.

LEFT MANY LOFTS, NOT MERELY THOSE DESIGNATED AS 'LIVE–WORK' SPACES, PROVIDE OPTIMUM CONDITIONS FOR WORKING FROM HOME. CHOOSE YOUR WORKING AREA CAREFULLY, PAYING ATTENTION TO ISSUES SUCH AS ACCESS, NATURAL LIGHT, SOUND LEVELS AND TECHNOLOGICAL INFRASTRUCTURE.

POINTS TO CONSIDER

- **Sound levels.** Do you prefer to work in absolute silence, or does the nature of your work require intense concentration? On the other hand, is your work inherently noisy? Do you make and receive phone calls, which may be distracting for people sharing the space? Acoustic panels or screens, or additional insulation may be the answer if you need to buffer out sound.

- **Light levels.** Some types of work are dependant on good natural light, particularly jobs which involve making fine colour judgements. Do artificial lighting arrangements support the type of work you do? Working on-screen, for example, requires a good level of diffused nondirectional background light: uplighting is ideal for this purpose. Daylight simulation bulbs can give a more natural level of light if you are working at some distance from a window.

- **Spatial requirements.** How much immediate desk space do you require? How much space does any equipment take up? What about storage for files and working materials?

- **Technological support.** Do you require additional phone lines or high-speed internet access? If space is tight, would it be possible to switch to a laptop rather than use a standard monitor? How much peripheral equipment do you require in the way of printers, faxes, scanners, and so on?

- **Access.** Do clients, customers or suppliers need to visit? If you are using a live–work space for this type of business, visits must be by appointment only. Can you arrange matters so that your workspace is directly accessible from the front door, or will visitors have to troop through your home to reach you?

- **Visibility.** Are you the type of person who can't switch off if their work remains on view? Do you need to maintain a professional image for clients or customers who may visit?

WORKSTATIONS

A workstation can be as impromptu and simple as a dining table, which is adequate for paying bills or the occasional day away from the office, but if you are serious about working from home you will need to set up a dedicated work zone. Precisely where depends largely on those factors highlighted above, but some degree of separation from the living space is generally a good idea. Make sure that your working area is out of main traffic routes.

Integrating a workstation within a sleeping area can make excellent sense in a loft, as sleeping areas are generally located away from the action and have a degree of privacy. Unless you regularly work into the small hours chasing deadlines, such an arrangement means that the space simply has two roles, a daytime function and a night-time function with a clear cut-off between the two.

Similarly, in a double-height space, setting up a working area on a mezzanine level can help to create a clear distinction between home and work life. Views are often beneficial for concentration and a desk that overlooks the rest of the space offers a good vantage point for creative daydreaming.

If you have little option but to site the workstation within the main living area, opt for a built-in arrangement. A working wall fitted with storage for files, cupboards and a long work surface can be screened from view by sliding panels, blinds (shades), drapes or bifolding doors when the time comes to stop work. Alternatively, spatial dividers, such as storage modules, can screen the space on a more permanent basis.

Keep basic furniture and fixtures simple and functional. Reclaimed office desks and filing cabinets, either stripped down to the bare metal or resprayed a vivid colour, suit the loft aesthetic. Mobile trolleys and computer stations that can be wheeled in and out of view are useful, though the need for access to power sources and phone lines might limit the mobile option to occasional computer

BELOW LEFT AND RIGHT **THIS WORKING WALL HOUSES A MATTRESS FOR FLOOR-LEVEL SLEEPING, A CLOSET FOR CLOTHES STORAGE AND A FULLY FITTED WORKSTATION, ALL BEHIND NEAT FLUSH PANELS.**

RIGHT **A MEZZANINE LEVEL IS OFTEN A GOOD PLACE TO SET UP A WORK AREA AS IT IS SITUATED OUT OF THE GENERAL RUN OF THE HOUSEHOLD. THIS DESK IS FURTHER SCREENED BY A CURTAIN.**

users. The new generation of 'office-in-a-box' work stations are ingenious designs that house a computer, desk space and storage for files within a large cupboard that closes completely to conceal all traces of work at the end of the day. Styles can be as ornate as a rustic armoires, but the clean lines of the more simple box designs will work well within a loft setting and will take their place happily in a streamlined storage system.

If your work involves sitting for long periods of time and working on-screen, invest in a good ergonomically designed chair – back pain is the most common work-related disorder and it can be very disabling. Chairs that offer adequate support for your back, which are fully adjustable to suit different heights and which can be tilted to follow different postures, will prevent you from stiffening up.

LEFT AND BELOW TWO VIEWS OF THE SAME SPACE SHOW A WORKING AREA SCREENED BY A LARGE FREE-STANDING WAIST-HEIGHT WOODEN PARTITION THAT DOUBLES AS A HEADBOARD FOR THE SLEEPING AREA ON THE OTHER SIDE. SUCH ARRANGEMENTS ARE IDEAL FOR PROMOTING THE CONCENTRATION REQUIRED FOR WORK AND FOR MAINTAINING THAT ALL-IMPORTANT PSYCHOLOGICAL SEPARATION OF DIFFERENT ACTIVITIES IN AN OTHERWISE OPEN SPACE.

case study

Flexibility is the key to a successful family home, both on a daily basis and in the longer term, as needs change and children grow. This conversion of a Victorian school in East Dulwich, London, into a home for an architect, his partner who designs textiles, and their young family, provides adaptable space to support a whole range of everyday activities without sacrificing the airy qualities of the original building.

The accommodation is arranged over three levels within the 7.5 m (25 ft) high space. On the lower level, there are open areas for cooking, dining, living, working and play. Custom-designed storage, sliding screens and shutters allows certain areas to be transformed as required.

The area immediately behind the kitchen, for example, is generally used as a play area. However, a large storage unit housing transparent boxes enables the space to be quickly cleared of toys when required. In the same area a filing cabinet/desk is fixed to the wall and is wired for telephone, fax, computer and hi-fi, which means the space can serve as an office in the evenings. And when guests come to stay, the full-height sliding screens can be pulled across to provide privacy and a futon pulled out from the storage unit, freeing up closet space.

The kitchen is generally open to the living area. However, it can also be closed off by means of sliding screens fitted to one side of the free-standing units, and with a long roller blind forming the third 'wall' adjacent to the main living space. This blind also acts as a projection screen, transforming the living area into a mini-cinema. The work surface of the tall unit can also be concealed behind up-and-over shutters when not in use.

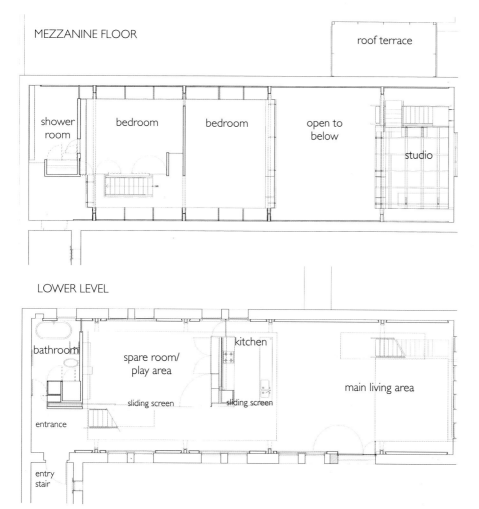

MEZZANINE FLOOR

roof terrace

shower room

bedroom

bedroom

open to below

studio

LOWER LEVEL

bathroom

spare room/ play area

kitchen

sliding screen

sliding screen

main living area

entrance

entry stair

LEFT: BY ADDING THE MEZZANINE LEVELS AN EXTRA 130 SQ M (1399 SQ FT) OF FLOOR AREA WAS PROVIDED.

RIGHT: OPEN TIMBER TREADS RISE UP FROM THE MAIN LIVING AREA ON THE LOWER LEVEL TO SERVE THE GLASS-FLOORED STUDIO. GLASS STAIRS ALSO PROVIDE ACCESS FROM THE MEZZANINE TO THE ROOF TERRACE. THE TRANSPARENT FLOOR AND STAIRS MAXIMIZE NATURAL LIGHT SPILLING DOWN THROUGH THE SKYLIGHTS. LIGHTING ARRANGEMENTS COMPLEMENT THE FLEXIBILITY OF THE LAYOUT. THE ENTIRE SPACE CAN BE EVENLY LIT TO ACCENTUATE THE SCALE OR INDIVIDUAL AREAS DIMMED AND CONTROLLED FOR GREATER INTIMACY. LIGHTING ALSO SERVES TO EMPHASIZE THE GLAZED PERIMETER OF THE MEZZANINES.

The middle level comprises two open platforms which overlook the main space below. One provides large sleeping and dressing areas, while the other is a working area and houses a textile studio. Both mezzanines appear to be held away from the walls by means of a glazed margin along the sides – this maintains the visual integrity of the existing building shell. The larger platform has a floor of birch-faced plywood and coir matting.

The studio floor is glass, allowing the light from the huge rooflight above to flood down into the area below.

The topmost level is above the larger mezzanine and provides two additional spaces, used as sleeping areas, attic play rooms or storage areas as required. The flexibility of the planning and arrangement means no space is wasted: the family use every single area on a daily basis.

ABOVE: THE LARGER OF THE TWO MEZZANINES HOUSES TWO GENEROUS SLEEPING AREAS. BOTH MEZZANINES ARE CONSTRUCTED IN SUCH A WAY AS TO AVOID INTERRUPTING VIEWS THROUGH THE SPACE AS LITTLE AS POSSIBLE. GLAZED MARGINS AT EITHER SIDE MEAN THAT THE LEVEL APPEARS TO BE INDEPENDENT OF THE MAIN WALLS. RADIATORS ARE RECESSED INTO THE LININGS OF THE SIDE WALLS.

ABOVE: WITH THE SHUTTERS OPEN, THE KITCHEN CAN BE SEEN IN ITS 'OPEN' POSITION. SLIDING PARTITIONS FITTED ALONGSIDE THE TALL UNITS, ALONG WITH A PULL-DOWN ROLLER BLIND, MEAN THAT THE ENTIRE AREA CAN BE COMPLETELY ENCLOSED IF REQUIRED.

LEFT: THE PLAY AREA/HOME OFFICE/GUEST ROOM IS LOCATED IMMEDIATELY BEHIND THE KITCHEN. NORMALLY KEPT FULLY OPEN, SLIDING DOORS CAN BE PULLED ACROSS TO PROVIDE PRIVACY. FLEXIBLE STORAGE HOUSES TOYS, FUTON AND OFFICE FILES.

Inside out

In many ways, the loft is the Great Indoors. Lofts and outdoor living are not obvious partners; the areas of the inner city where warehouses, factories and workshops have been recycled as hip new living spaces tend to be low on amenities of a more conventional domestic nature, such as garden space. It is well to accept that if you live in a loft you can forget any notions about lovingly tending acres of green lawn or indulging a passion for a herbaceous border. But that does not mean that you have to turn your back on the outside world or exist in a nature-free zone.

Lofts which obviously offer the greatest scope for outdoor living are those with access to roof terraces, or those on the ground level adjoining a communal yard or outdoor area. In between, it may be a question of exploiting windowsills to the full, or investigating the possibility of adding a balcony to extend the living space outside.

ROOF GARDENS

Roof terraces and gardens are among the most dramatic of all outdoor areas. If you have a loft on the top floor of a building, but don't have a terrace, it can be worth sacrificing a little floor area to make an outdoor space. Roof terraces not only offer sweeping views of the cityscape – especially thrilling on a warm summer's evening – but they also have that extra frisson of the unexpected. Something about seeing plants growing high up off the ground is utterly captivating.

If roof gardens are particularly dramatic, they are also quite demanding areas to cultivate. Conditions can be extreme: full exposure to scorching sun and also strong winds and rain. Not all plants will tolerate a rooftop location and you will probably need to provide some degree of shelter to mitigate the swings of temperature and humidity, as well as protection from the wind. Trellising or some form of fencing around the perimeter can make all the difference, both to your enjoyment of a roof terrace and the variety of plants you will be able to grow.

If the roof is particularly exposed, and especially if it is overlooked, perimeter fencing or enclosure is recommended. Roof gardens tend

to attract attention and you may need to shield yourself from inquisitive eyes. By the same token, safety is also a prime consideration. Make sure walls and parapets are built up to a sufficient height, particularly if children will be using the space.

Before you begin to plan a roof garden or terrace, you will need advice from a surveyor to determine the strength of the roof structure itself. The combined weight of containers, planting medium and plants can impose significant extra loads, as can any decking or flooring material you may wish to lay to make the space more attractive, practical or comfortable. Think about drainage, too. Make sure there is some way that water can run off from pots rather than resting on the surface and causing potential damp problems.

Planting will, to some extent, be dictated by rooftop conditions. Spiky or architectural plants, such as bamboo, palms and various types of grasses, avoid any hint of quaintness and will cope with desiccating winds. Climbers can be successfully grown up trellises and container herb gardens will supply fresh flavours for the table all year round.

ABOVE **AN ARRAY OF TERRACOTTA POTS AND A FEW CLIMBERS TRANSFORMS A ROOF TERRACE INTO A HIGH-RISE URBAN GARDEN. ROOF-TOP CONDITIONS CAN BE EXTREME, SO CHOOSE PLANTS WHICH CAN TOLERATE THE EXPOSURE.**

RIGHT **NOT SO MUCH A ROOF GARDEN AS A FULLY FURNISHED OUTDOOR ROOM, THIS LUXURIOUS AND INVITING TERRACE PROVIDES A SECLUDED PLACE FOR RELAXING, EATING AND ENTERTAINING OUT IN THE FRESH AIR.**

Roof terraces not only offer sweeping views of the cityscape – especially thrilling on a warm summer's evening – but they also have that extra frisson of the unexpected.

BALCONIES

Balconies do not have to be extensive to offer the benefits of outdoor space. Enough room for a few pots, a table and a couple of chairs will allow you to soak up the sun or eat alfresco, weather permitting. The wall of the building will offer some shelter, particularly from strong winds, as well as a handy surface for anchoring climbing plants. As with roof terraces, you may need to check with a surveyor to ensure that an existing balcony is strong enough to support additional loading from pots and furniture.

INTERIOR GARDENS

If you have no access to an outdoor area, however limited, you can still bring nature indoors. Like anything else you put into a loft, scale is a prime consideration. Standard houseplants won't do the trick, particularly if your loft has very high ceilings. Think about exotic plants or small containers of trees of the type grown in atria, which will provide the height and impact you need in a big space. Really large or luxuriant plants can also act as spatial dividers. Another strategy is to group pots so that you create what is effectively an indoor garden with its own microclimate. Select species that require the same conditions in terms of natural light and humidity and group them where conditions are optimal.

An alternative route, which has become popular in recent years, is to create natural displays out of found materials, such as shells, beach pebbles, twigs and driftwood. Again, be wholehearted about such displays: a few lone pebbles strewn around can look a little precious and contrived, whereas a huge section of a tree branch with an interesting form can be as arresting as a piece of sculpture.

At the very least, lofts present an ideal context for displays of cut flowers and foliage. An array of delicate glass containers, each holding a single bloom, can be arranged along the length of a glass shelf or in front of a window, or a huge bunch of larkspur, stocks or cheerful sunflowers placed in a prominent position. These ideas help to keep a sense of nature alive, even in the most urban of surroundings.

BELOW AND RIGHT **ACCESS TO OUTDOOR SPACE PROVIDES A WHOLE NEW DIMENSION TO LOFT LIVING. THIS ROOF TERRACE IN MANHATTAN FEATURES CONTRASTING MATERIALS UNDERFOOT – PAVING AND PEBBLES – WITH PLANTERS AND CONTAINERIZED FLOWERS.**

OVERLEAF **THE USE OF CONTRASTING MATERIALS CAN EVOKE A NATURAL ENVIRONMENT. THIS ROOF-TOP SUNTRAP IS BORDERED BY GRAVEL WHICH IS PLANTED WITH HARDY SPECIES. THE MAIN SURFACE IS WOODEN DECKING; THE LOUNGERS ARE MADE OF CONCRETE.**

case study

One solution for those in lofts with no terrace is to add a balcony. As this scheme shows, the result is more successful when like-minded neighbours join forces to employ a professional designer.

The neighbours live on three different floors of a warehouse in south London, which was once used to store Bibles. Independently, all three had been thinking about adding a deck or balcony to provide space for outdoor living but were daunted by the related structural and planning issues. Once they joined forces and hired an architectural practice, however, they were able to realize their plans in a more considered fashion than if they had proceeded separately.

When it comes to adding on a balcony, the chief structural issue is whether the existing external walls can bear the load.

In this case, the architects came up with the idea of a lightweight steel-framed structure, rather like free-standing shelving, which is bolted onto the wall of the warehouse. Most of the load of the structure, however, is carried on the front steel columns, which makes it a much more practical and achievable solution. Each balcony comprises a deck 9m (30 ft) long by 3m (10 ft) wide, adding nearly 300 sq m (3,228 sq ft) of usable living space to each loft. The only other structural work was creating new openings between the lofts and balconies.

The balconies face south, benefiting from good light. On the top level, there is an electrically operated canvas roof shade to keep off the glare of the sun; on windy days, it automatically retracts. Frosted glass panels fixed to the balustrading let in light but screen views. These are arranged differently on each balcony according to aspect and level of light. Equally important, the frosted panels help to solve the main issue as far as gaining planning permission is concerned, which is being overlooked – careful positioning of the balconies and placement of the frosted glass screens overcame any potential objections from neighbouring properties. The result has been a three-way transformation, both indoors and out.

RIGHT: THE TOP-FLOOR BALCONY, WITH ITS ELECTRICALLY OPERATED SHADE, PROVIDES AN OUTDOOR ROOM PROTECTED FROM THE ELEMENTS. FROSTED GLASS PANELS SCREEN VIEWS AND ALLOW PRIVACY.

BELOW, LEFT AND RIGHT: THE THREE BALCONIES WERE DESIGNED AS A BOLT-ON STRUCTURE FIXED TO THE EXTERNAL WALLS BUT SUPPORTED ON THE FRONT COLUMNS.

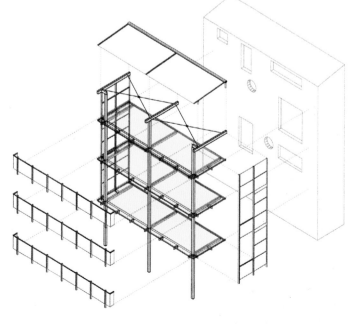

case study

Tucked away in an alleyway in Pigalle, this conversion of an old workshop is nothing less than a green oasis in the heart of Paris. The owner, who already had a home in the area, stumbled upon the abandoned building when he was looking for an office near where he lived. Smitten by the atmosphere of the ancient alleyway and the unique wooden facade of the workshop, which had once housed part of an old theatre, Théatre Andre-Antoine, he decided to take the whole building, installing his office on the first floor and making a home for himself on the ground floor.

Although the place was completely derelict and had to be rebuilt from scratch, the owner was not daunted by the task. As the son and brother of architects, building sites were no mystery to him and he applied himself to the task of designing the plans and supervizing the works.

Converting the ground floor of the building into a home took a year. Comprising 100 sq m (1,076 sq ft) of floor area, the apartment is essentially three linked spaces, each of which opens onto a small square patio. Disliking the formal separation of doors, and wishing to bring as much light as possible into what had been a fairly dark building, the owner designed the layout so that different areas are separated from one another by partitions of various heights. Separating the bedroom from the area set aside for reading and study, for example, is a partly open divider which provides shelves for books as well as storage for clothes. It is positioned in such a way as to allow a direct view of the patio from the bed.

In keeping with the wooden facade of the building, a unifying theme of the decoration of the apartment is mahogany panelling, which is used to clad walls and storage units. Mahogany-faced panels conceal all the working elements of the apartment, from radiators and kitchen appliances to the washing machine and drier.

The use of mahogany and other natural materials in the decoration also helps to emphasize the true charm of the loft, which is its ready connection with outdoors. The luxuriant planting of the patio is visible from all areas via large wood-framed windows that bathe the space in light.

RIGHT AND FAR RIGHT: THE DINING AREA OPENS DIRECTLY ON TO THE SMALL, SQUARE, LUXURIANTLY PLANTED PATIO – THE HEART OF THE LOFT.

OVERLEAF: THE MAIN LIVING AREA, WITH THE DINING AREA IN THE BACKGROUND, IS BATHED IN NATURAL LIGHT. A HUGE MIRROR ON THE FLANKING WALL REFLECTS MORE LIGHT INTO THE SPACE. CURTAINS (DRAPES), BOTH AT THE WINDOWS AND THOSE USED TO SEPARATE DIFFERENT AREAS WITHIN THE APARTMENT, ARE MADE FROM NATURAL LINEN.

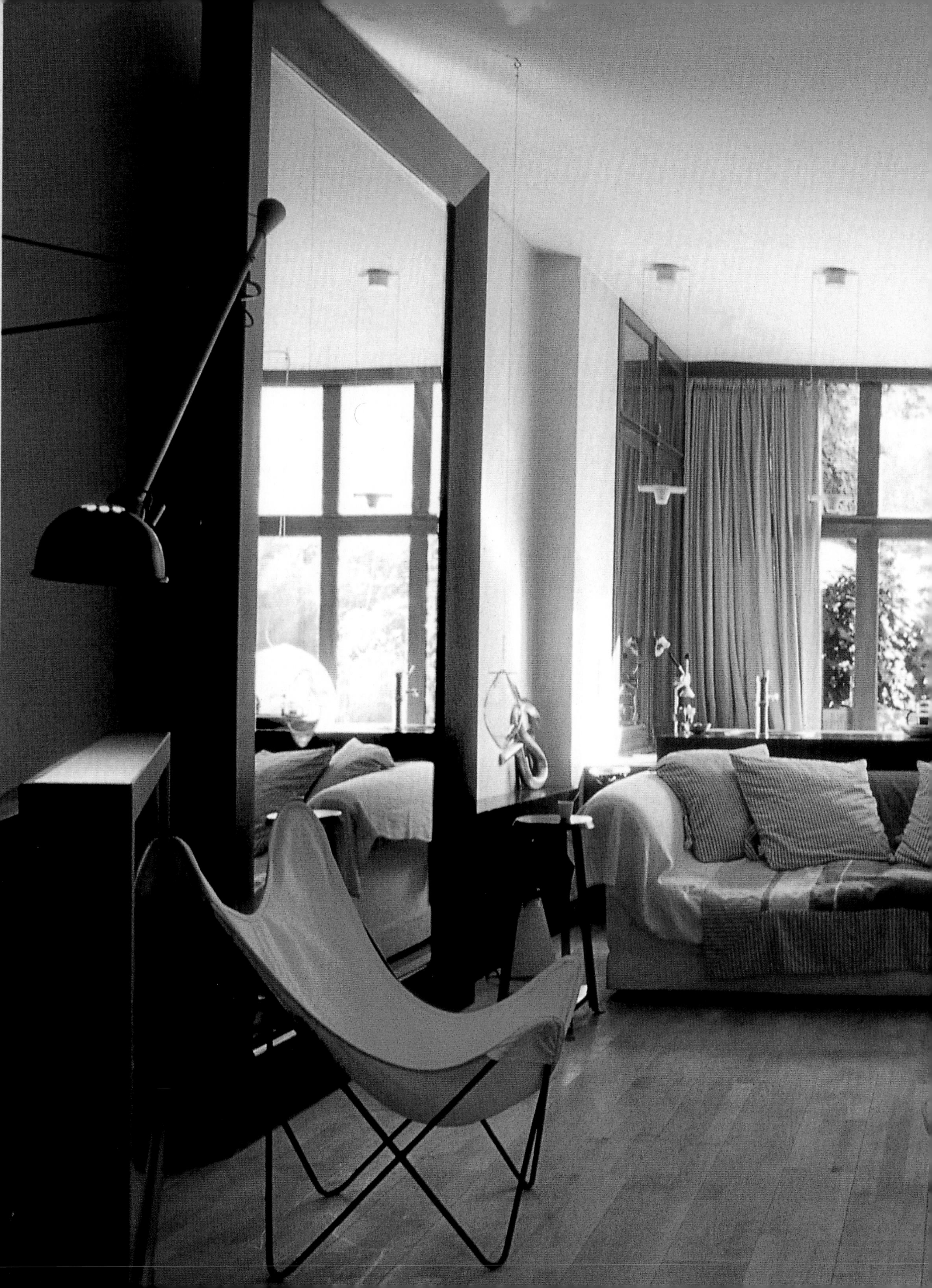

RIGHT: THE READING CORNER IS MINIMALLY FURNISHED WITH AN OAK AND CHESTNUT WOOD BENCH DESIGNED BY CHRISTIAN LIAGRE AND A LE CORBUSIER DAY BED COVERED IN LEATHER.

FAR RIGHT: THE BEDROOM IS SCREENED FROM THE READING CORNER BY A MAHOGANY DIVIDER, WHICH HOUSES SHELVES FOR BOOKS AND CLOTHES. THE PANELLING ON THE WALLS IS ALSO MAHOGANY. THERE IS A VIEW OF THE PATIO FROM THE BED.

BELOW: THE PATIO, ACCESSED FROM ALL THE PRINCIPAL LIVING AREAS, BRINGS A SENSE OF NATURE INDOORS.

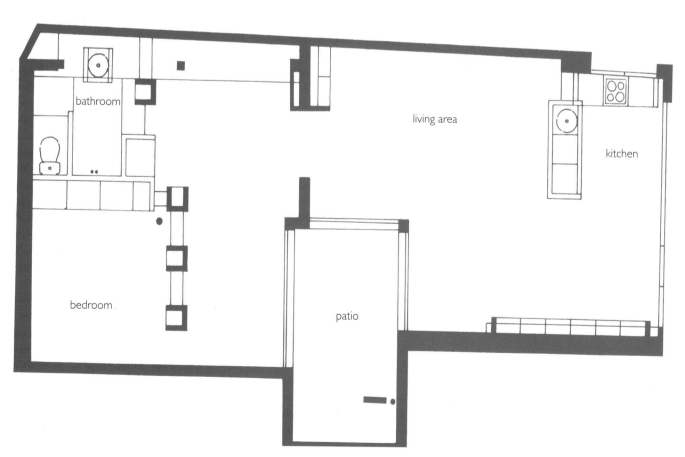

bathroom

living area

kitchen

bedroom

patio

Resources

FABRICS & WALL COVERINGS

Barsouv
91 Orchard St.
New York, NY 10002
212.925.3400

Circle Fabrics
263 W. 38th St.
New York, NY 10018
212.719.5153

Donghia
979 3rd Ave.
New York, NY 10022
212.935.3712
(to the trade)

J. Robert Scott
500 N. Oak St.
Inglewood, CA 90302
310.680.4300
(to the trade)

Nobilis, Inc.
973 3rd Ave.
New York, NY 10022
212.980.1177
(to the trade)

METAL WORK

Edelman Metalworks
9 State St.
Danbury, CT 06810
203.744.7331

Jeff Mase
39 9th Ave.
New York, NY 10014
212.929.1289

LEATHERGOODS

Libra Leather, Inc.
259 W. 30th St.
New York, NY 10001
212.695.3114

Renar
68 Spring St.
New York, NY 10012
212.349.2075

WINDOW TREATMENTS, CURTAINS & BLINDS

Allstate Glass
85 Kenmare St.
New York, NY 10012
212.226.2517

George Molina
100 Emerson Pl.
Brooklyn, NY 11205
718.789.3190
Curtains, drapes, upholstery

FLOORING

American Olean
    Tile Company
100 Cannon Ave.
Lansdale, PA 19446
215.855.1111

Architectural Systems
150 W. 25th St.
New York, NY 10001
212.206.1730
Multipurpose flooring

DWF (Designer
    Wood Flooring)
446 W. 38th St.
New York, NY 10018
212.971.0226

Kentucky Wood Floor
P.O. Box 33726
Louisville, KY 40232
800.235.5235

Perfect Circle Studios
64 Jay St.
Brooklyn, NY 11201
718.643.0244
Stainless steel flooring tiles

DECORATIVE PAINT & MATERIALS

Bendheim Glass
122 Hudson St.
New York, NY 10013
212.226.6370
Glass and glass cubes

Cesar Color Inc.
4625 S. 32nd St.
Phoenix, AZ 85040
602.243.1434
Glass

John Depp
41–40 38th St.
Long Island City, NY 11101
718.784.8500
Glass, mirror

Foro
140 3rd St.
Brooklyn, NY 11231
718.852.2322
Marble

Fresco
324 Lafayette St.
New York, NY 10012
212.966.0676

Joanne Hudson Assoc. Ltd
The Marketplace Design Center
2400 Market St., Suite 310
Philadelphia, PA 19103
800.217.7931

Renfrow Tile
1822 Sunnyside Ave.
Charlotte, NC 28204
704.334.6811
Marble, glass tile

Chris Townley
208 Bowery
New York, NY 10012
212.941.1606
Plaster

LIGHTING

Cooper Lighting
P.O. Box 4446
Houston, TX 77210
713.739.5400

Donzella 20th Century
17 White St.
New York, NY 10013
212.965.8919

Flos, Inc.
200 McKay Rd.
Huntington Station, NY 11746
516.549.2745
(to the trade)

Fontana Arte
8807 Beverly Blvd.
Los Angeles, CA 90048
310.247.9933

Ideas & Products
31 S. 5th Ave.
Tucson, AZ 85716
520.791.9267

Lighting By Gregory
158 Bowery
New York, NY 10012
212.226.1276

Luceplan USA
315 Hudson St.
New York, NY 10013
212.691.8263
(to the trade)

Urban Archeology Co.
143 Franklin St.
New York, NY 10013
212.431.4646

Villa Lighting
1218 S. Vandeventer
St. Louis, MO 63110
800.325.0963

KITCHEN & BATH

AF Supply
22 W. 21 St.
New York, NY 10010
212.243.5400

Bowery Discount Hardware
& Restaurant Supply
105 Bowery
New York, NY 10002
212.966.6375
Kitchen

The Chicago Faucet Co.
2100 S. Nuclear Dr.
Des Plaines, IL 60018
847.803.5000

George Taylor Specialties
100 Hudson St.
New York, NY 10013
212.226.5369

JADO Bath & Hardware
Mfg. Co.
1690 Calle Quetzal
Camarillo, CA 93011
805.482.2666

Kohler Co.
Design Center
101 Upper Rd.
Kohler, WI 53044
920.457.3699

Waterworks
469 Broome St.
New York, NY 10013
212.966.0605
Bathroom

FURNITURE &
ACCESSORIES

ABC Carpet & Home
888 Broadway
New York, NY 10003
212.473.3000

Aero
132 Spring St.
New York, NY 10012
212.966.1500

BDDW
8 Rivington St.
New York, NY 10002
212.228.7322
Furniture, lighting, design

Coconut Company
131 Greene St.
New York, NY 10012
212.539.1940

Domestic Furniture
6150 Wilshire Blvd.
Los Angeles, CA 90036
323.936.8206

Form & Function
95 Vandam St.
New York, NY 10013
212.414.1800

Global Table
187 Sullivan St.
New York, NY 10012
212.431.5839

Holly Hunt
979 3rd Ave.
New York, NY 10022
212.755.6555
(to the trade)

Jet Age Studio
250 Oak St.
San Francisco, CA 94102
415.864.1950

Knoll
105 Wooster St.
New York, NY 10012
212.343.4102
(to the trade)

Lin Weinberg
84 Wooster St.
New York, NY 10012
212.219.3022

Dennis Miller Associates
306 E. 61st St.
New York, NY 10021
212.355.4550
(to the trade)

M2L
979 3rd Ave.
New York, NY 10022
212.832.8222
(to the trade)

Modern Living
8775 Beverly Blvd.
Los Angeles, CA 90048
310.657.8557

Moss
146 Greene St.
New York, NY 10012
212.219.3022

Pucci International
44 W. 18th St.
New York, NY 10011
212.633.0452

Marc O. Rabun
Art & Antiques
115 Crosby St.
New York, NY 10012
212.226.5053

Totem Design
71 Franklin St.
New York, NY 10013
212.463.8910

Troy
138 Greene St.
New York, NY 10012
212.941.4777

280 Modern
280 Layfayette St.
New York, NY 10012
212.941.5825

Vintage Modern Gallery
1515 N. Central Ave.
Phoenix, AZ 85004
602.462.5790

Wyeth
151 Franklin St.
New York, NY 10013
212.925.5278

ARCHITECTURAL
SALVAGE

Demolition Depot
216 E. 125th St
New York, NY 10035
212.860.1138

Renovator's Supply
Renovator's Old Mill
Millers Falls, MA 01349
800.659.2211

Wooden Nickel Antiques
1410 Central Parkway
Cincinnati, OH 45210
513.241.2985

CARPET & RUGS

Dolma
417 Lafayette, 2nd Fl.
New York, NY 10003
212.460.5525

Einstein Moomjy Inc.
150 E. 58th St.
New York, NY 10155
212.758.0980

Mark Shilen
109 Greene St.
New York, NY 10012
212.925.3394

WEBSITES

www.interiorinternet.com
www.furniture.com
www.internetdesigncenter.com
www.lampa.com
www.totemdesign.com
www.industrial-home.com
www.rabidhome.com

Index

Acknowledgements

Page 1 View / Richard Glover / Arthur Collin Architects, page 2 Carlton Books / Chris Brooks / Hanrahan Meyers Architects, page 3 Jam Factory / Ian Simpson Architects, page 4 Verne, page 5 Carlton Books / Chris Brooks / Rogers Marvel Architects, page 6 Carlton Books / Chris Brooks / Rogers Marvel Architects, page 7 Camera Press / Max Jourdan, page 9 Richard Powers, page 10 Richard Powers, Page 13 Courtesy Manhattan Loft Corporation, page 14–15 Ray Main / Mainstream / McDowell & Benedetti Architects, page 16 Courtesy Manhattan Loft Corporation, page 18 Carlton Books / Chris Brooks / Hanrahan Meyers Architects, page 19 Courtesy Abelow Connors Sherman Architects, page 21 Courtesy Manhattan Loft Corporation, page 23 top and bottom Project Orange Architects, page 24–5 Paul Warchol, page 26 Narratives / Jan Baldwin, page 27 Carlton Books / Chris Brooks / Rogers Marvel Architects, page 28 Courtesy Simon Condor Architects, page 29 Camera Press / Max Jourdan, page 31 Nicole Rowntree, page 32 top and bottom Nicole Rowntree, page 33 Nicole Rowntree, page 34 Verne, page 35 Verne, page 36 Verne, page 37 Verne, page 38–9 Verne, page 40 Courtesy Manhattan Loft Corporation, page 41 View / Peter Cook, page 42 Courtesy de Metz Architects, page 43 Courtesy Brookes Stacey Randall Architects, page 44 Courtesy Histon Allvey Architects, page 45 Courtesy Histon Allvey Architects, page 46 Jeremy Young, page 47 Jeremy Young, page 48 Ray Main / Mainstream / Designers Collett-Zarzycki, page 49 Ray Main / Mainstream / Designers Collett-Zarzycki, page 50 Ray Main / Mainstream / McDowell & Benedetti Architects, page 51 Carlton Books / Chris Brooks / Dive Architects, page 52 Courtesy Q Property Ltd / John Kerr Associates, page 53 Courtesy Q Property Ltd / John Kerr Associates, page 54 Courtesy Q Property Ltd, page 57 Courtesy Knight Frank, page 58–9 Carlton Books / Chris Brooks / Hanrahan Meyers Architects, page 61 Carlton Books / Chris Tubbs / Christoff:Finio Architecture, page 62 arcblue / Jefferson Smith / Dive Architects, page 63 Carlton Books / Chris Brooks / Dive Architects, page 64–5 View / Millennium lofts / Dennis Gilbert, page 66 Carlton Books / Chris Brooks / Dive Architects, page 67 Carlton Books / Chris Brooks / Rogers Marvel Architects, page 68 top Carlton Books / Chris Brooks / Rogers Marvel Architects, bottom arcblue / Jefferson Smith, page 69 Courtesy Simon Condor Architects, page 71 top and bottom Courtesy Block Architecture, page 75 left and right Courtesy Block Architecture, page 73 Courtesy Block Architecture, page 74 Richard Powers, page 76 Courtesy Project Orange, page 77 top arcblue / Jefferson Smith, bottom Courtesy Project Orange, page 78 Yoo Building (London) Courtesy Yoo Ltd, page 79 left Courtesy de Metz Architects, right Carlton Books / Chris Tubbs / Christoff:Finio Architecture, page 80 left Ray Main / Mainstream / McDowell & Benedetti middle View / Arthur Collin Architect / Richard Glover, page 81 Carlton Books / Chris Tubbs / Christoff:Finio Architecture, page 82 top Carlton Books / Chris Brooks / Rogers Marvel Architects bottom Chris Tubbs, page 83 View / Chris Gascoigne, page 84 top Carlton Books / Chris Brooks / Rogers Marvel bottom Christoph Kicherer, page 85 View / Chris Gascoigne, page 86 Michael Moran / Archi-Tectonics, NY, page 87 Paul Warchol, page 88 Carlton Books / Chris Brooks / Dive Architects, Page 89 Courtesy Stone Paper Knife, Page 90 Chris Tubbs, page 91 top Carlton Books / Graham Atkins-Hughes, bottom Carlton Books / Chris Brooks, page 92 Chris Tubbs, page 93 top Carlton Books /

Chris Brooks / Hanrahan Meyers Architects bottom Carlton Books / Chris Brooks / Hanrahan Meyers Architects, page 94 Mikkel Vang, page 95 Mikkel Vang, page 96 Mikkel Vang, page 97 Mikkel Vang, page 98 Mikkel Vang, page 99 top and bottom Mikkel Vang, page 100 Ray Main / Mainstream, page 103 Ray Main / Mainstream, page 104 Ray Main / Mainstream, page 105 Ray Main / Mainstream, page 107 Elle Decoration UK / Stefano Azario, page 108 left and right Elle Decoration UK / Stefano Azario, page 109 Elle Decoration UK / Stefano Azario, page 110 Paul Warchol, page 111 Paul Warchol, page 113 Paul Warchol, page 114 Chris Tubbs, page 115 Ray Main / Mainstream page 116 Carlton Books / Chris Brooks / Michael Davis Architects, page 116–17 Carlton Books / Chris Brooks / Michael Davis Architects, page 118 Carlton Books / Chris Brooks / Michael Davis Architects, page 119 left and right Carlton Books / Chris Brooks / Michael Davis Architects, page 120–1 arcblue / Jefferson Smith, page 122 Carlton Books / Chris Tubbs / Christoff:Finio Architecture, page 123 Carlton Books / Chris Tubbs / Christoff:Finio Architecture, page 124 Ray Main / Mainstream, page 125 top Carlton Books / Chris Brooks / Hanrahan Meyers Architects, 125 bottom View / Dennis Gilbert, page 126 Chris Brooks / Hanrahan Meyers Architects, page 127 Arc Blue / Jefferson Smith / Dive Architects, page 129 top and bottom de Metz Architects, page 130 Ray Main / Mainstream, page 131 left and right Ray Main / Mainstream, bottom Arcaid, page 132 Verne, page 134 left and right Chris Tubbs, page 135 Narratives / Jan Baldwin, page 136 Verne, page 137 Verne, page 139 James Macmillan / Courtesy Brookes Stacey Randall Architects, page 140 James Macmillan / Courtesy Brookes Stacey Randall Architects, page 141 James Macmillan / Courtesy Brookes Stacey Randall Architects, page 142 Carlton Books / Chris Brooks, page 143 Carlton Books / Chris Brooks / Rogers Marvel Architects, page 144 left and right Carlton Books / Chris Brooks / Rogers Marvel Architects, 145 Carlton Books / Chris Brooks / Rogers Marvel Architects, page 146–7 Richard Powers, page 148 Courtesy Form Architects / page 149 Courtesy Form Architects, page 150 Red Cover / Nicolas Millet / Maison Francais, page 151 Red Cover / Nicolas Millet / Maison Francais, page 152–3 Red Cover / Nicolas Millet / Maison Francais, page 154 Red Cover / Nicolas Millet / Maison Francais, page 155 Red Cover / Nicolas Millet / Maison Francais

Every effort has been made to acknowledge correctly and contact the source and/or copyright holder of each picture and Carlton Books Limited apologizes for any unintentional errors or omissions which will be corrected in future editions of this book.

Special thanks to:
Eugene Colberg, Martin Finio, Michael Davis, Christopher Chew, Ia Hjärre, Andy Nettleton and all the architects who kindly assisted with the making of this book.